AF225982

Two Dads, Two Daughters

Four Generations of Art

E. C. Flickinger

Sarah F. Wimberley

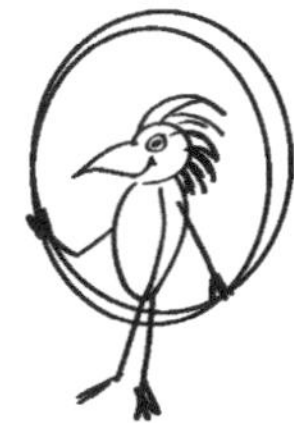

A Grackle Book

Grackle Publishing - Ambler, Pennsylvania

Grackle

An imprint of Grackle Publishing, LLC

gracklepublishing.com

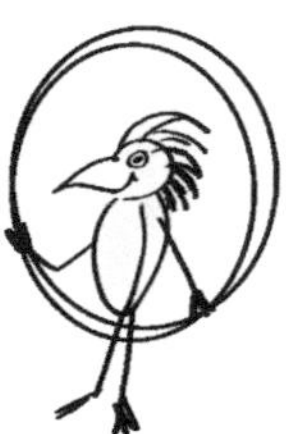

Library of Congress Control Number: 2019939036

ISBN: 978-0-9982069-4-3

Four Generations of Art

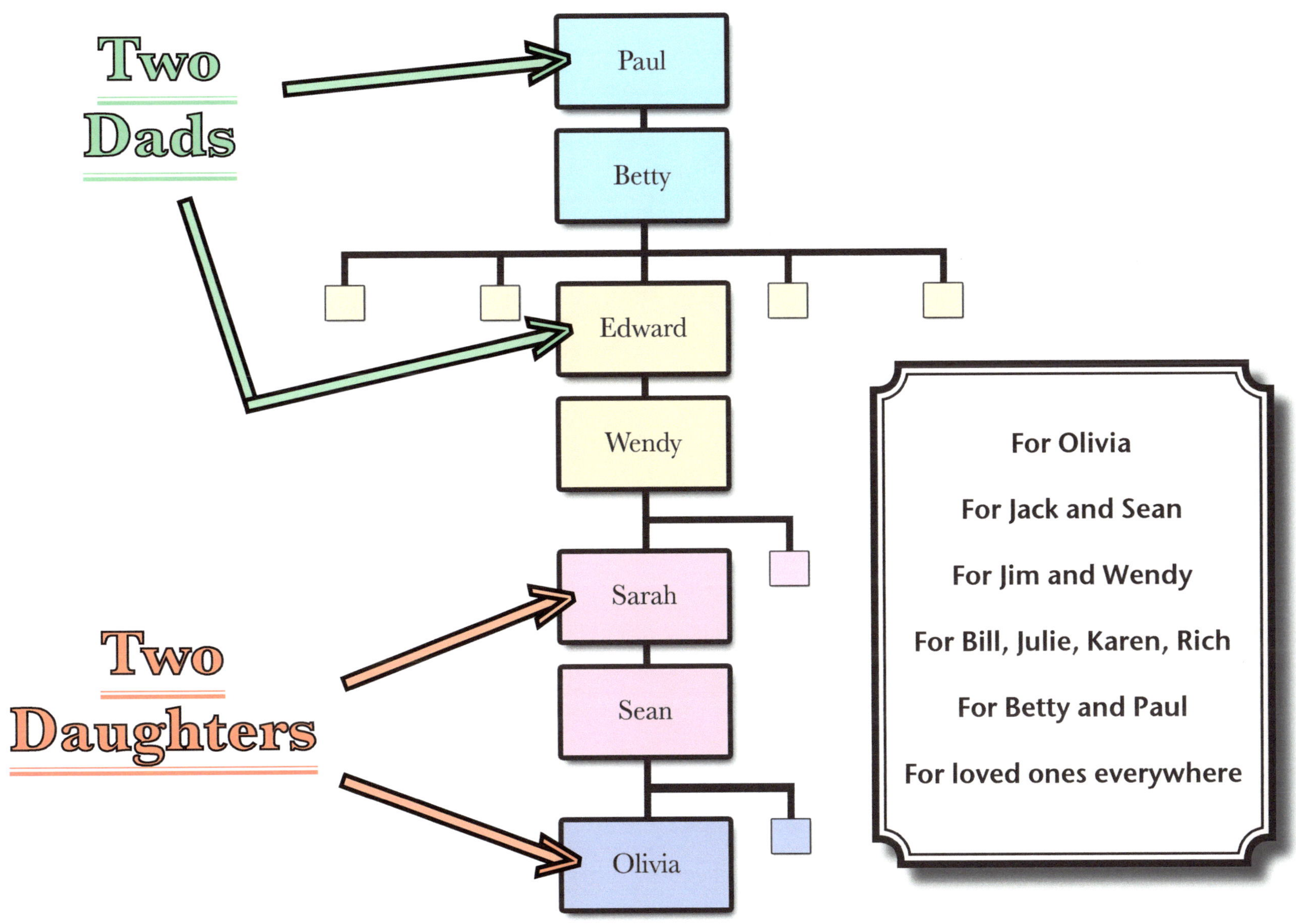

Shapes

Children love creating art with shapes. Here Olivia gives life to a friendly frog who is very happy to meet you.

Adults love shapes too as you will soon see when we are "knee-deep" in all kinds of serious shapes.

Watch for the frog to find Olivia's art!

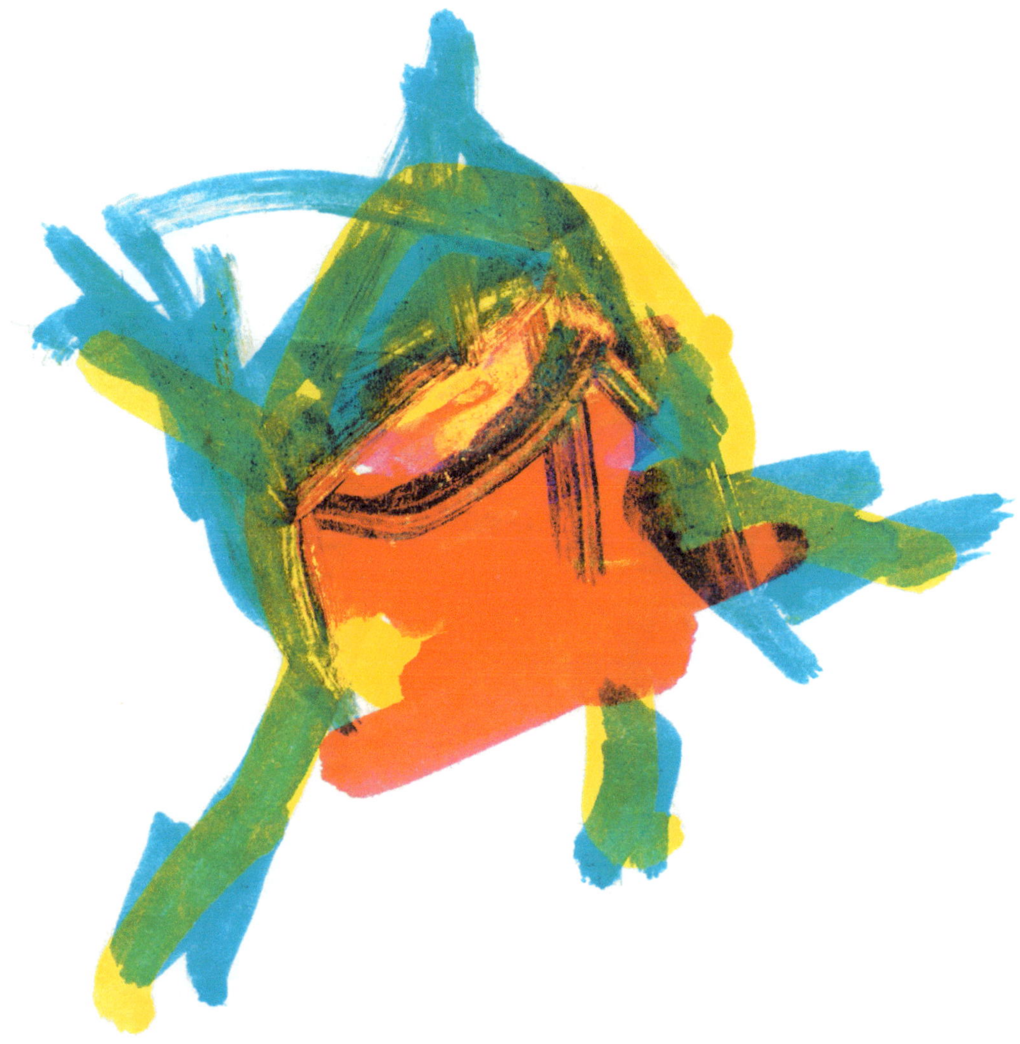

Olivia M. Wimberley
Frog, 2017
Watercolor on paper, 3 x 3 inches
Age 3

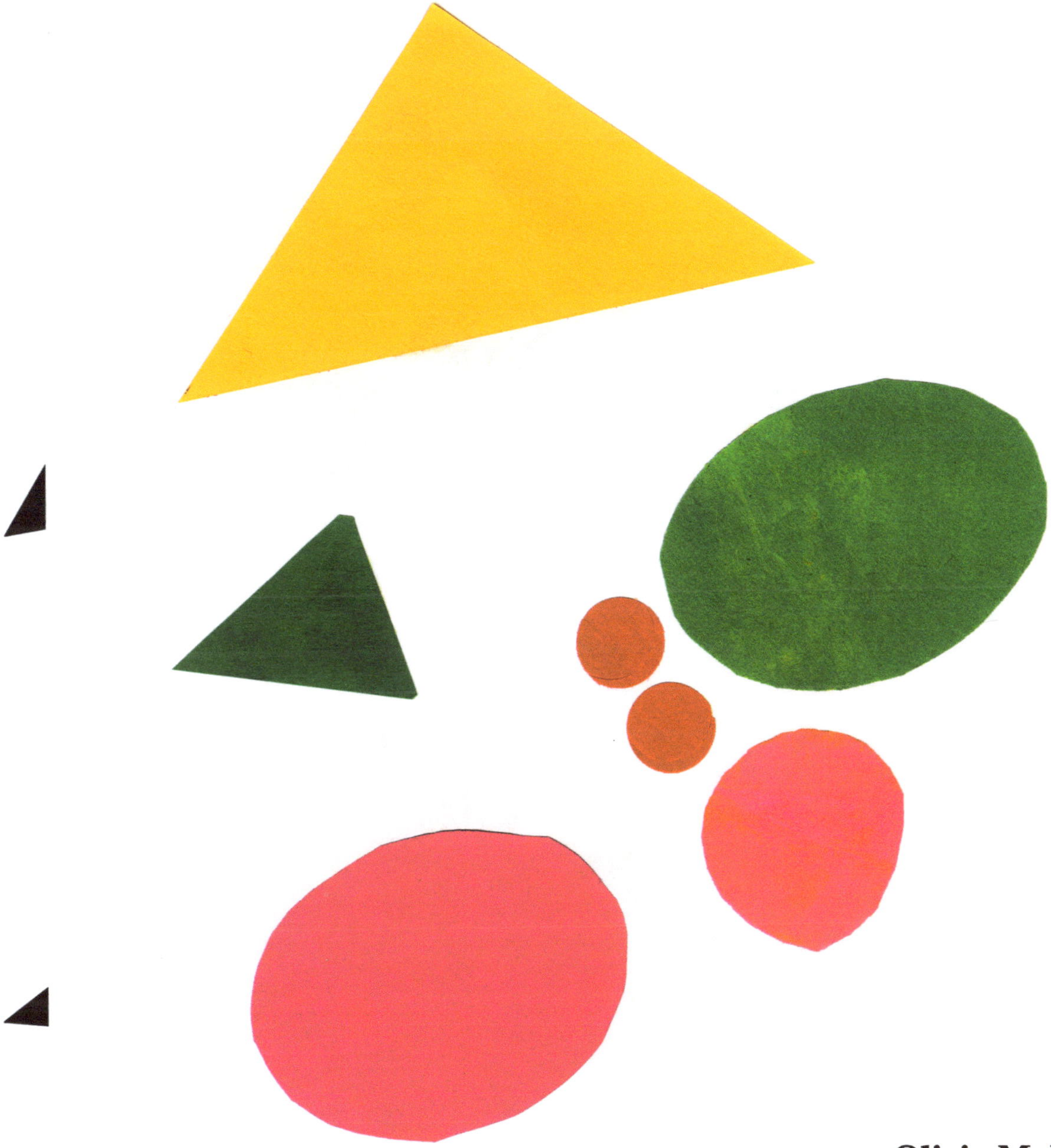

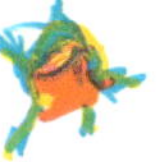

Olivia M. Wimberley
Shapes, 2017
Collage, 9 x 11 inches
Age 2

5

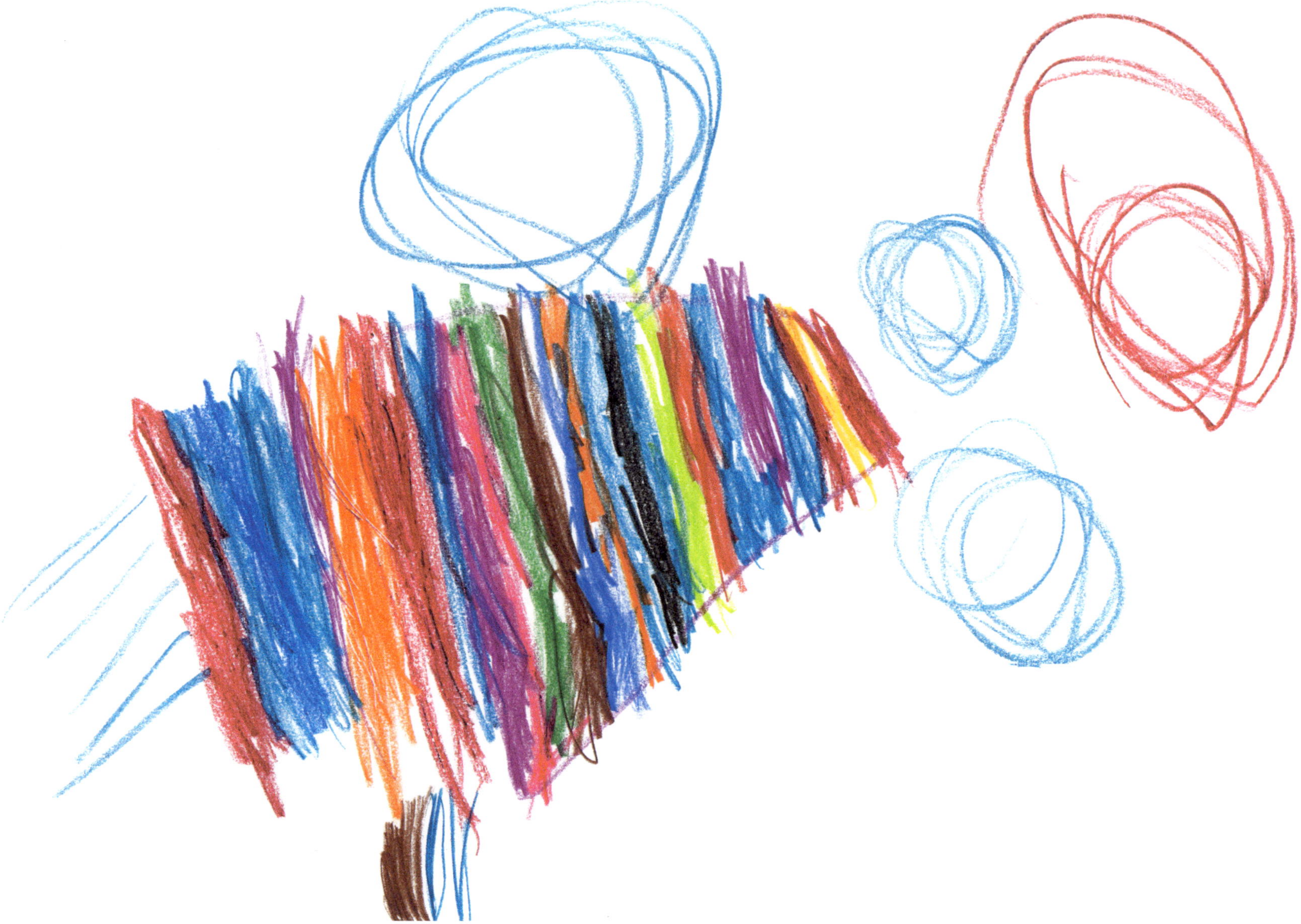

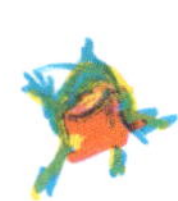

Olivia M. Wimberley
New Year's Eve (As the Ball Fell), 2018
Crayon on paper, 22 x 16 inches
Age 4

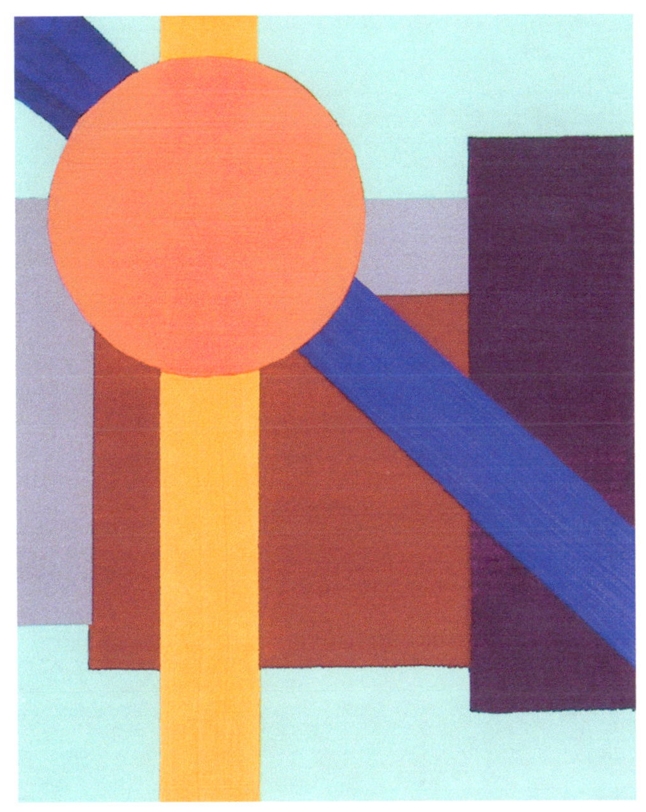

Sarah F. Wimberley
Brighter Than The Sun, 2004
Acrylic on paper
11 x 14 inches

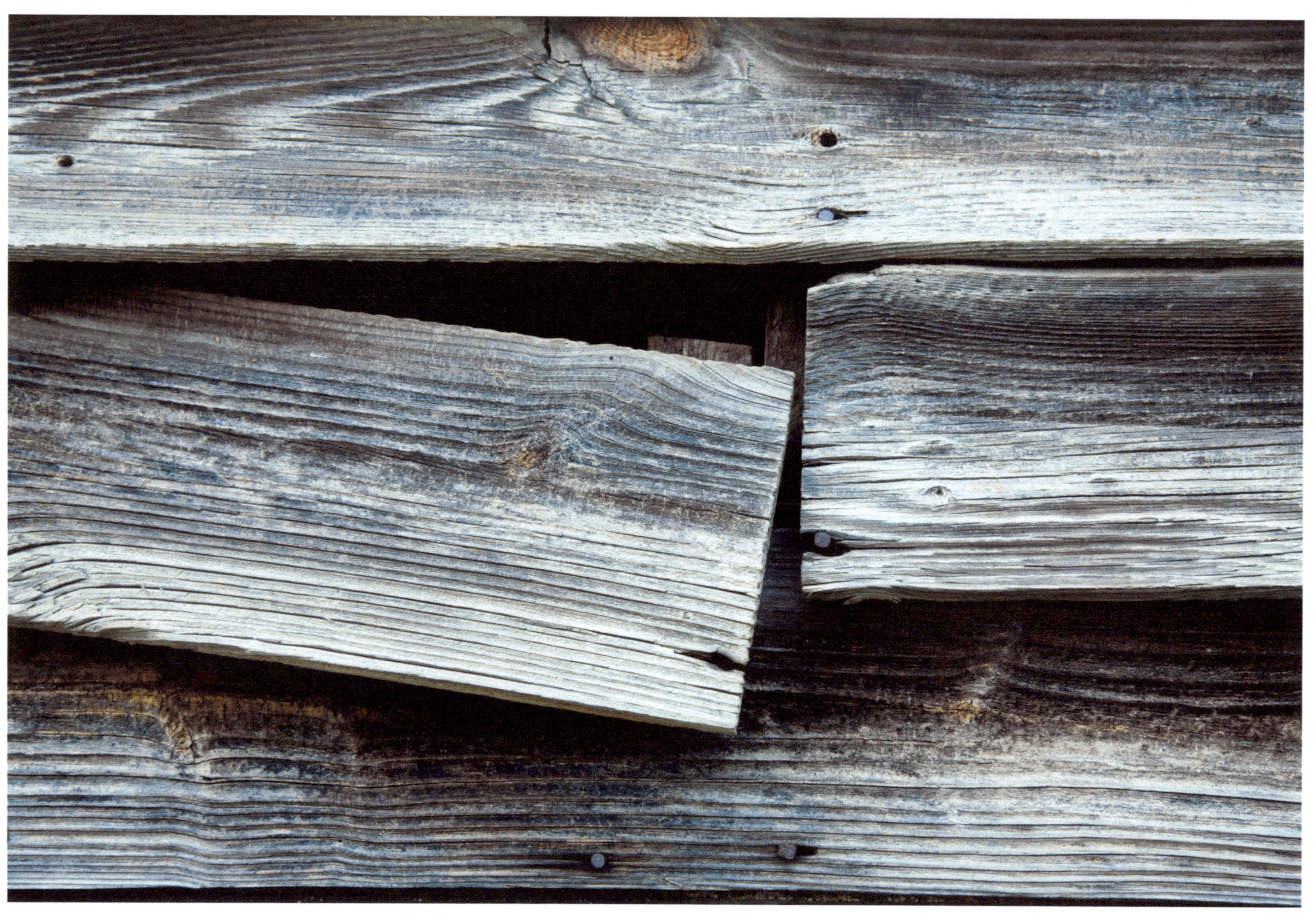

Sarah F. Wimberley
The Barn Where Buchanan Slept, 2007
Digital photography
Norlina, Warren County, NC

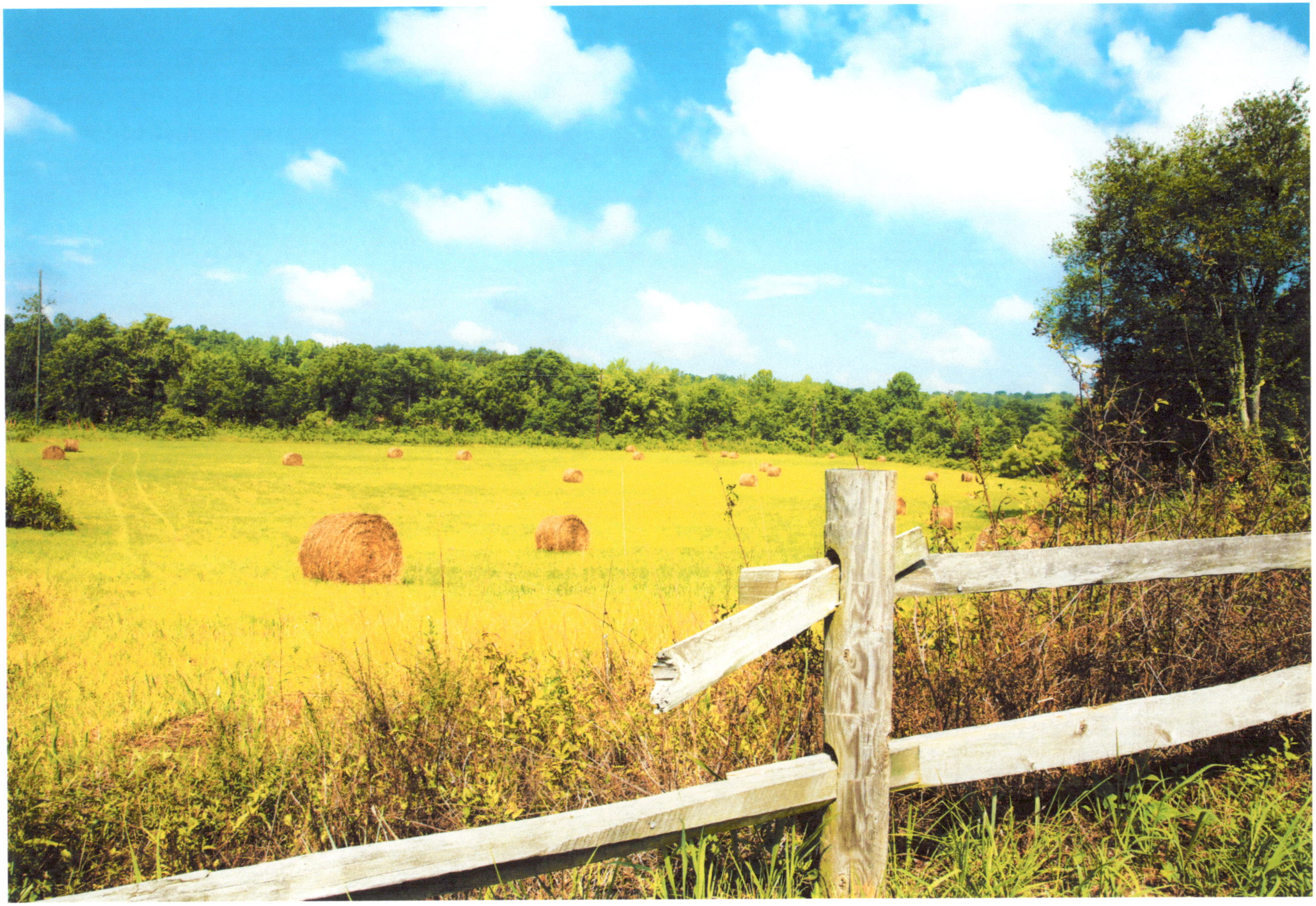

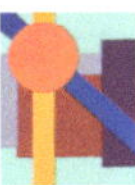

Sarah F. Wimberley
Unnamed Highway Farm, 2007
Digital photography
Connelly Springs, Burke County, NC

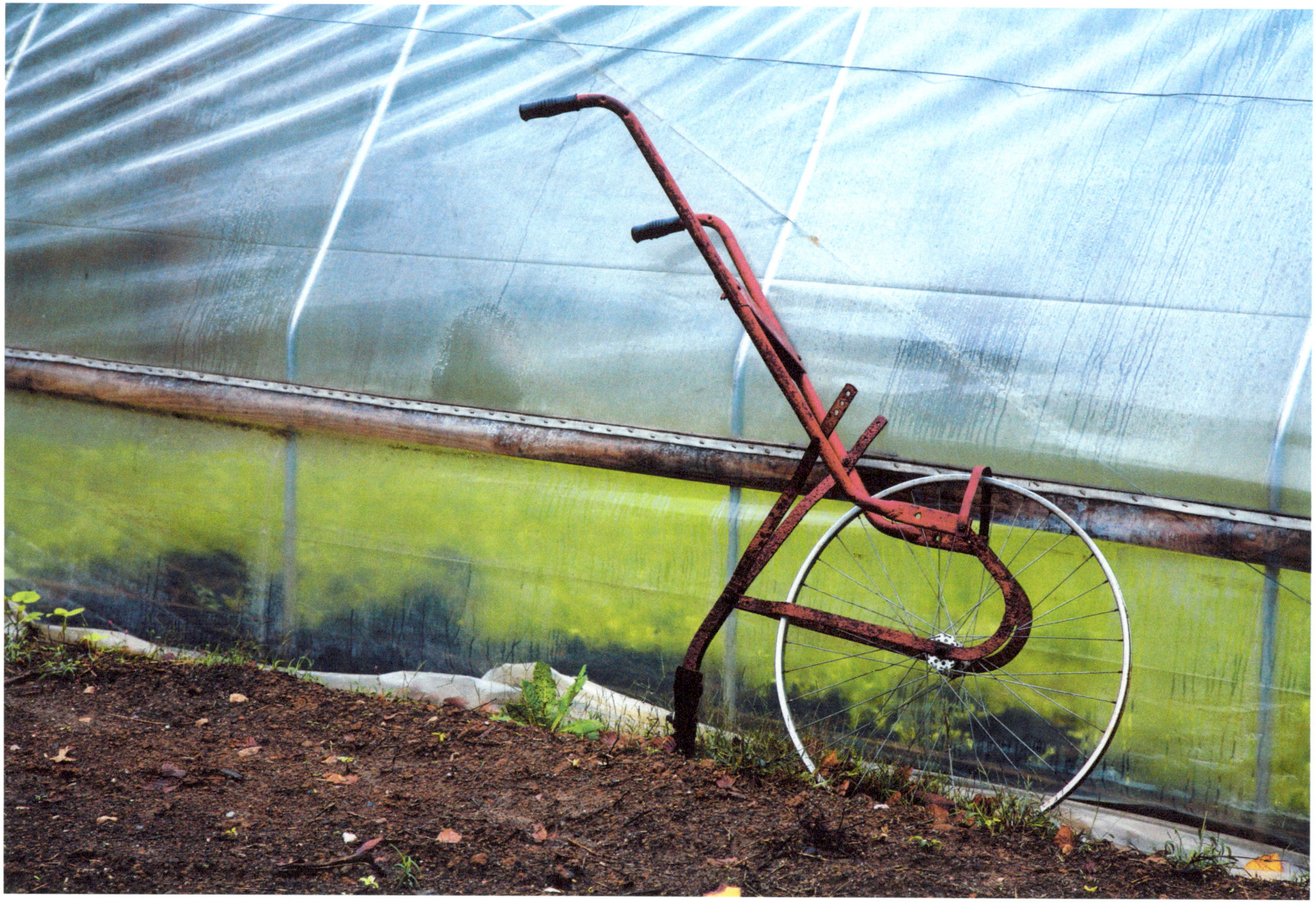

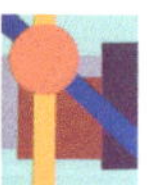

Sarah F. Wimberley
Shiitake Mushroom Farm, c. 2007
Digital photography
Browns Summit, Guilford County, NC

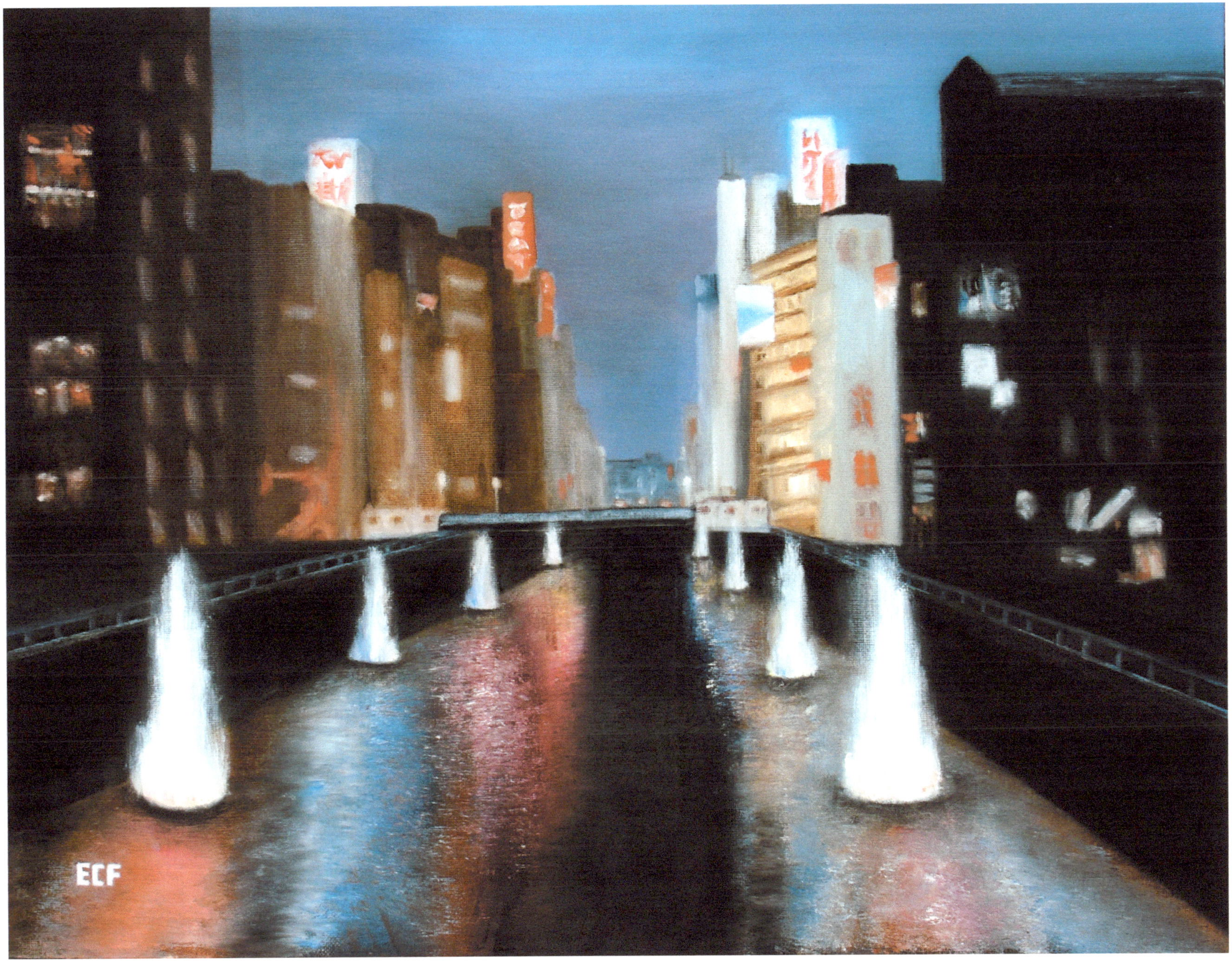

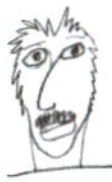

E. C. Flickinger, *Osaka*, 2006
Oil on canvas, 20 x 16 inches, evening view of Dōtonbori, Osaka, Japan, c. 1990

11

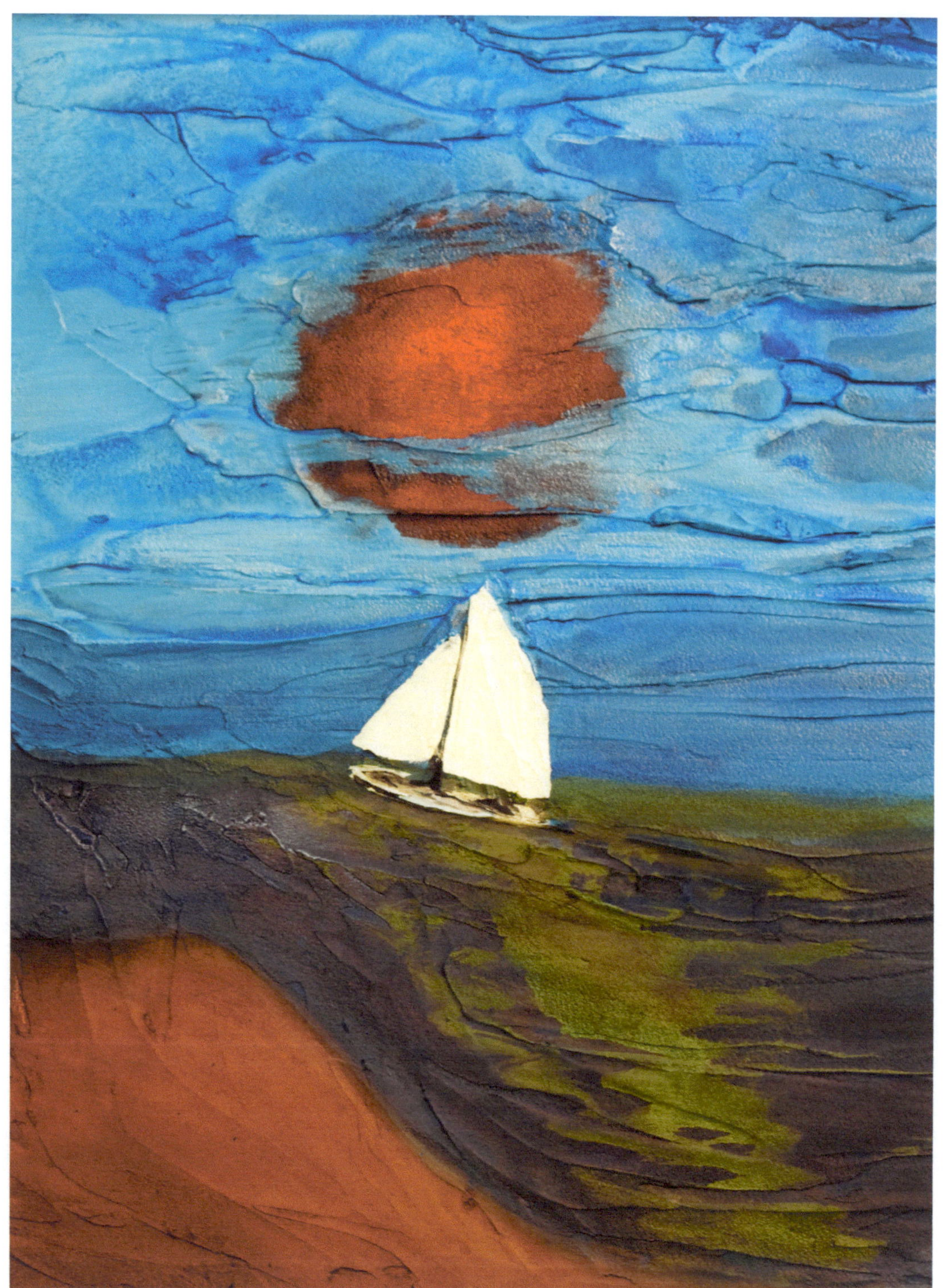

E. C. Flickinger
Three Hour Tour, 2008
Mixed media, 10 x 13 inches
Destiny steers the end of a
Three Hour Tour.

Soloist

Inspired by Picasso

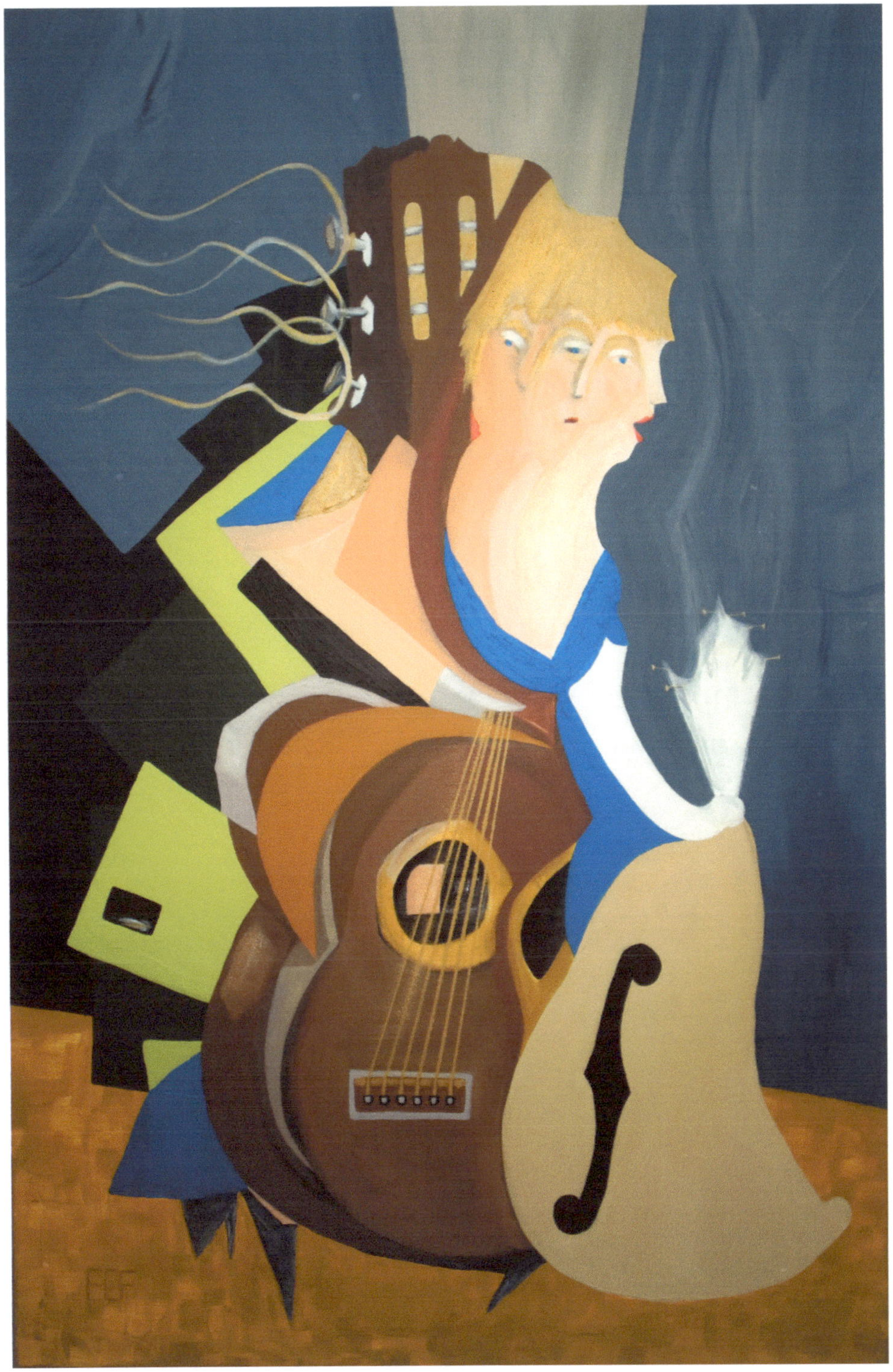

E. C. Flickinger
Soloist, 2010
Acrylic on canvas, 24 x 36 inches
Inspired by Picasso's
paint-like-a-child method.

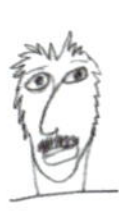

13

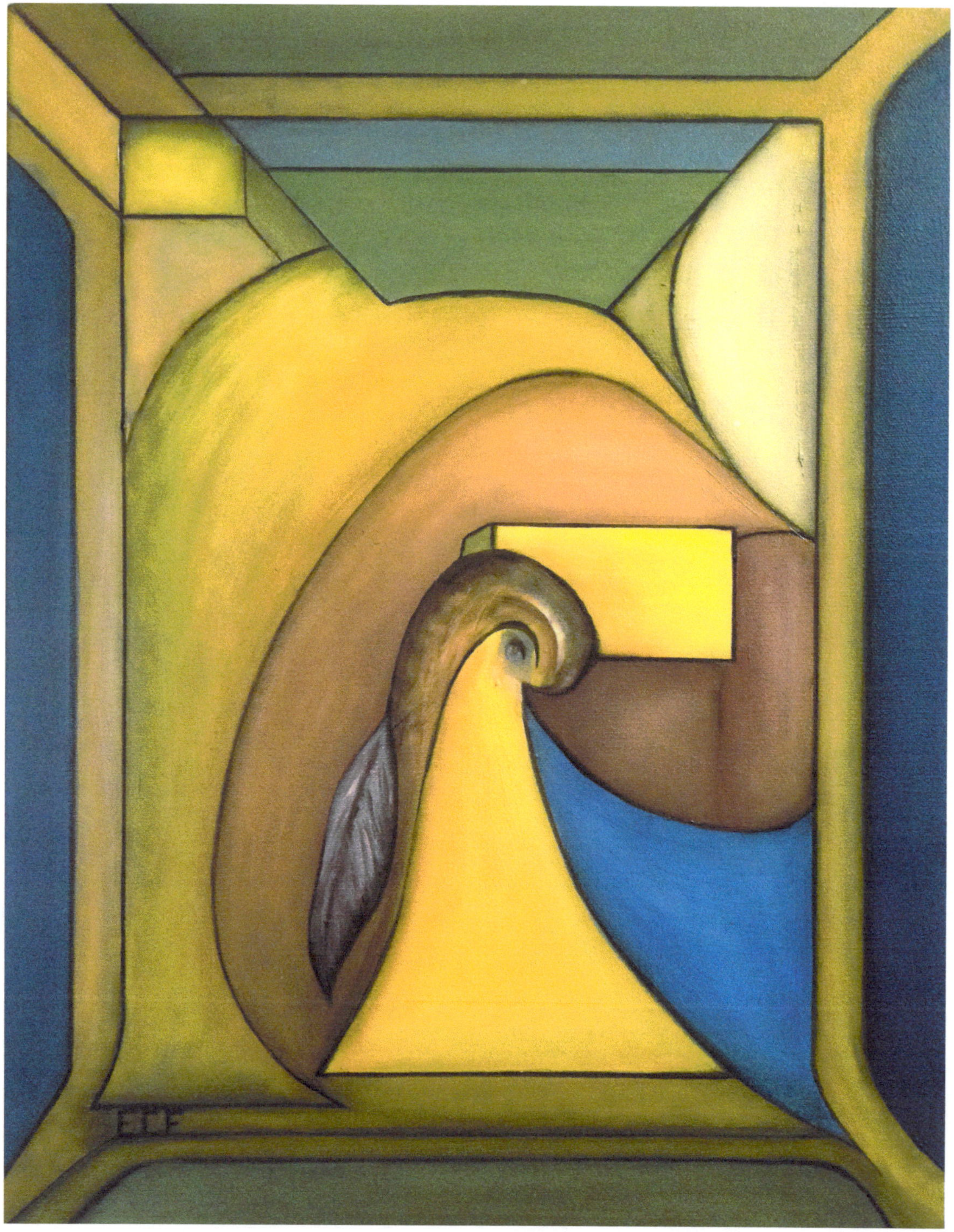

The Cold

Makes me hold
my goose down,
run blindly
through the woods—
...

Is it better to divide
by zero than live
in obscurity?

Sorry to ask again,
the cold
makes me forget.

—ECF

E. C. Flickinger
Missing Peace, 2016
Oil on canvas, 16 x 20 inches
Monument for battles
better not fought.

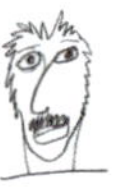

Do You Remember...

The first time we kissed?

The love and the bliss?

Our first embrace?

How our hearts did race?

If you remember,

Then you will know

Why I still love you so.

–Paul

Paul H. Flickinger, Jr.
Treasured Memories
c. 1978
Acrylic on canvas
12 x 16 inches

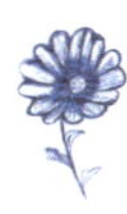

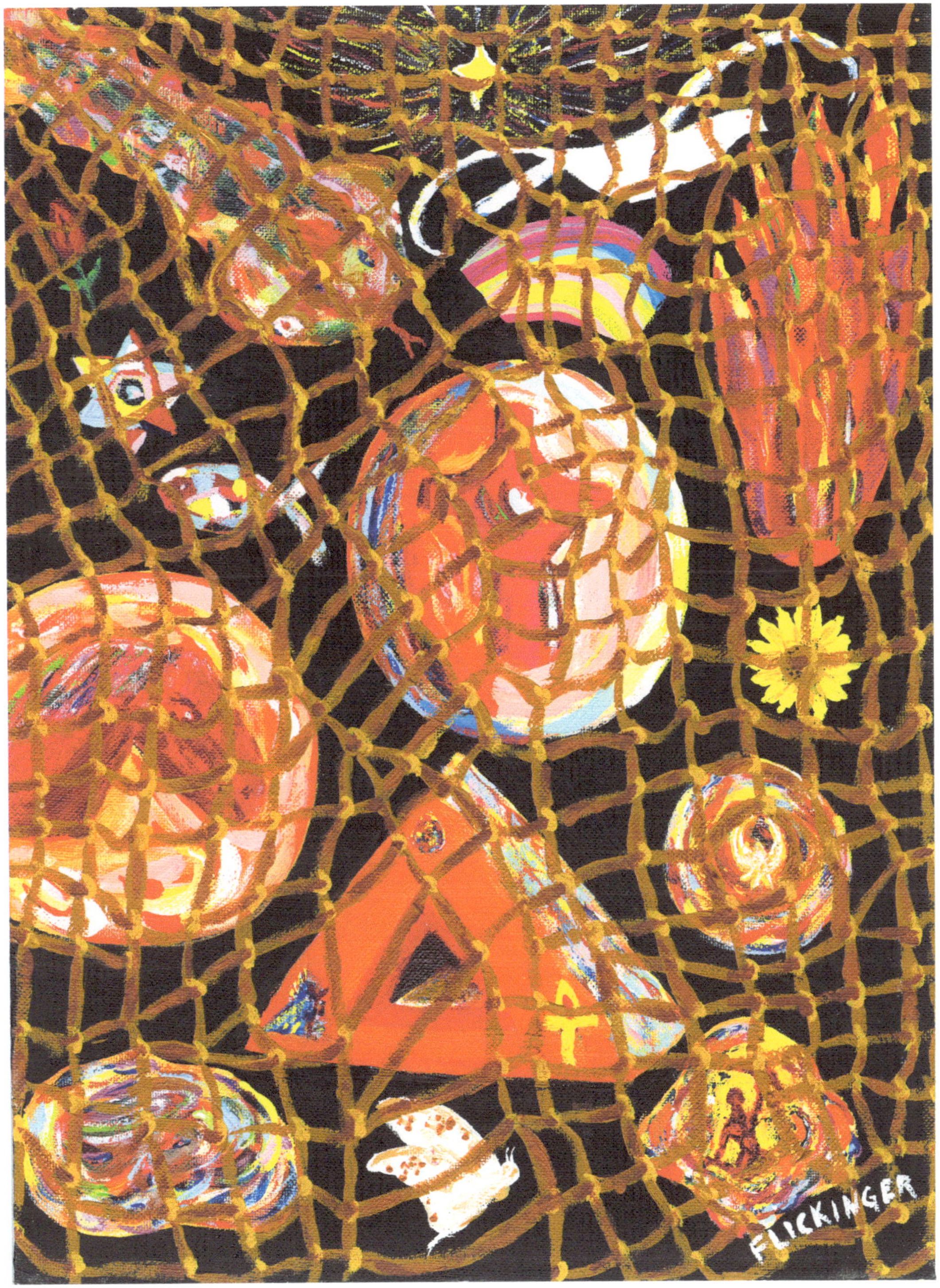

Drawings

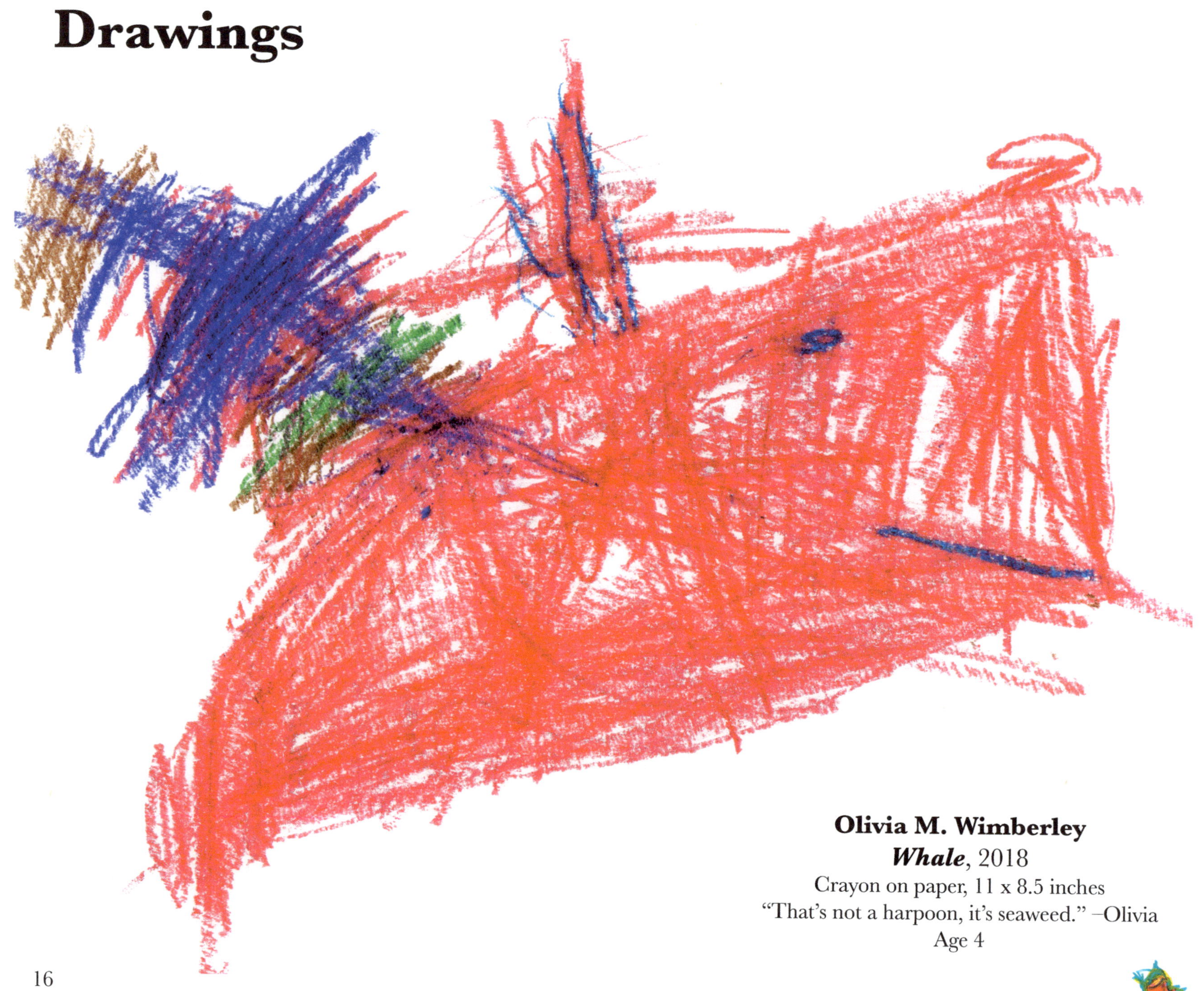

Olivia M. Wimberley
Whale, 2018
Crayon on paper, 11 x 8.5 inches
"That's not a harpoon, it's seaweed." –Olivia
Age 4

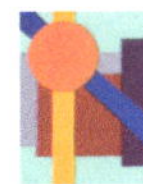

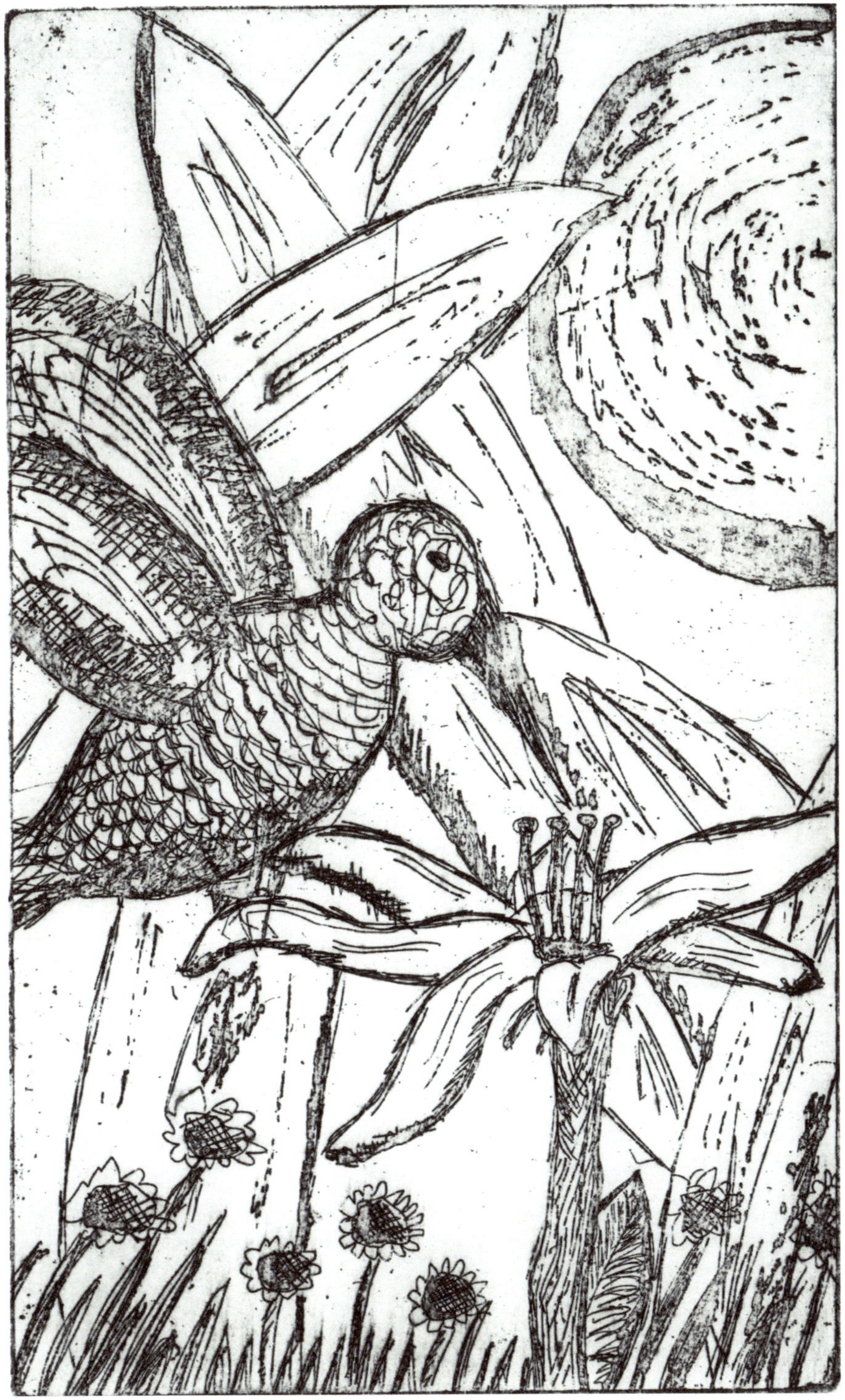

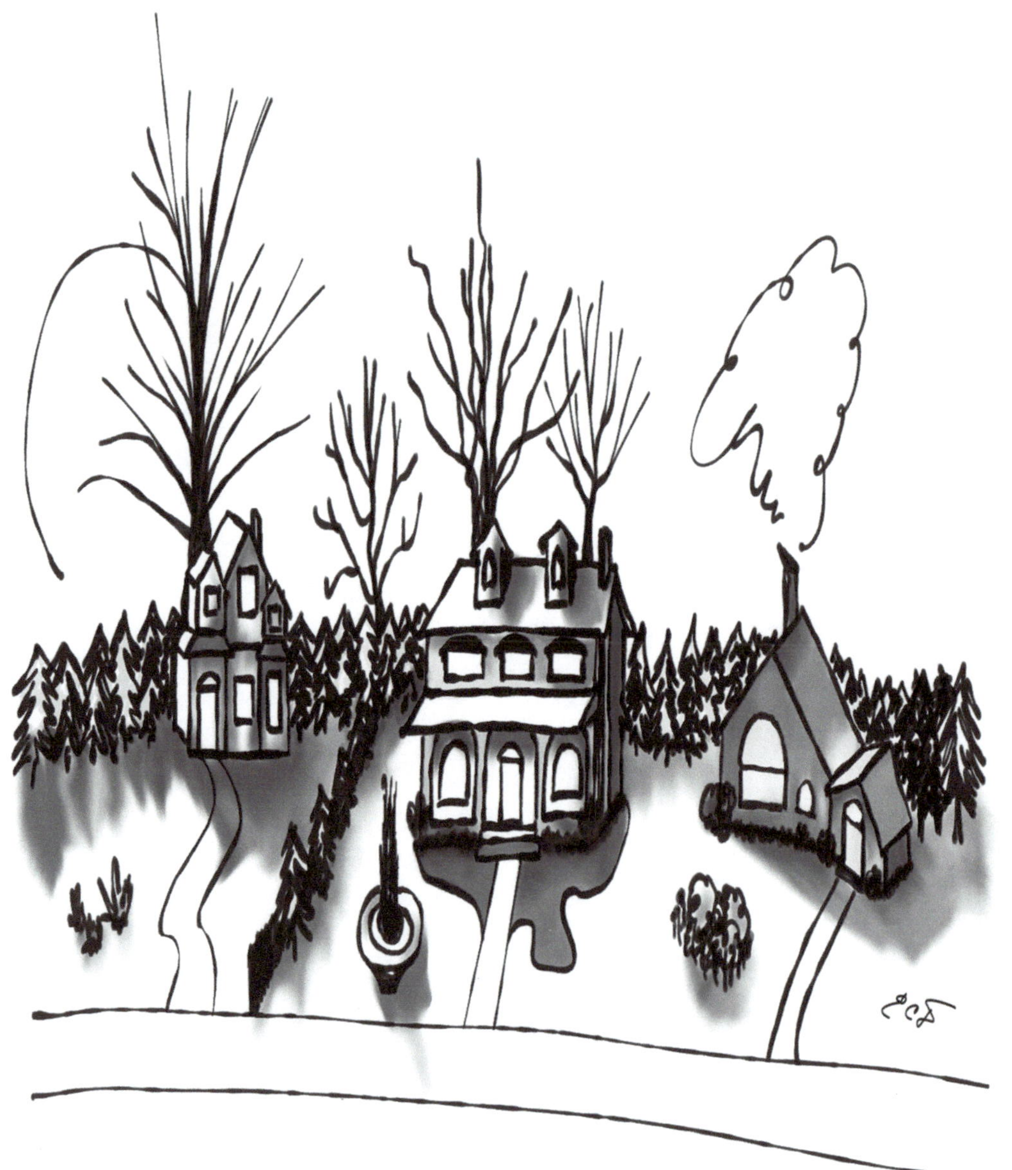

E. C. Flickinger
Pine Avenue, 2017
Digital pen and ink

Nolava

K. S. Lee

Pine Avenue and *House on the Hill* will be featured in K. S. Lee's forthcoming novel, *Nolava*.

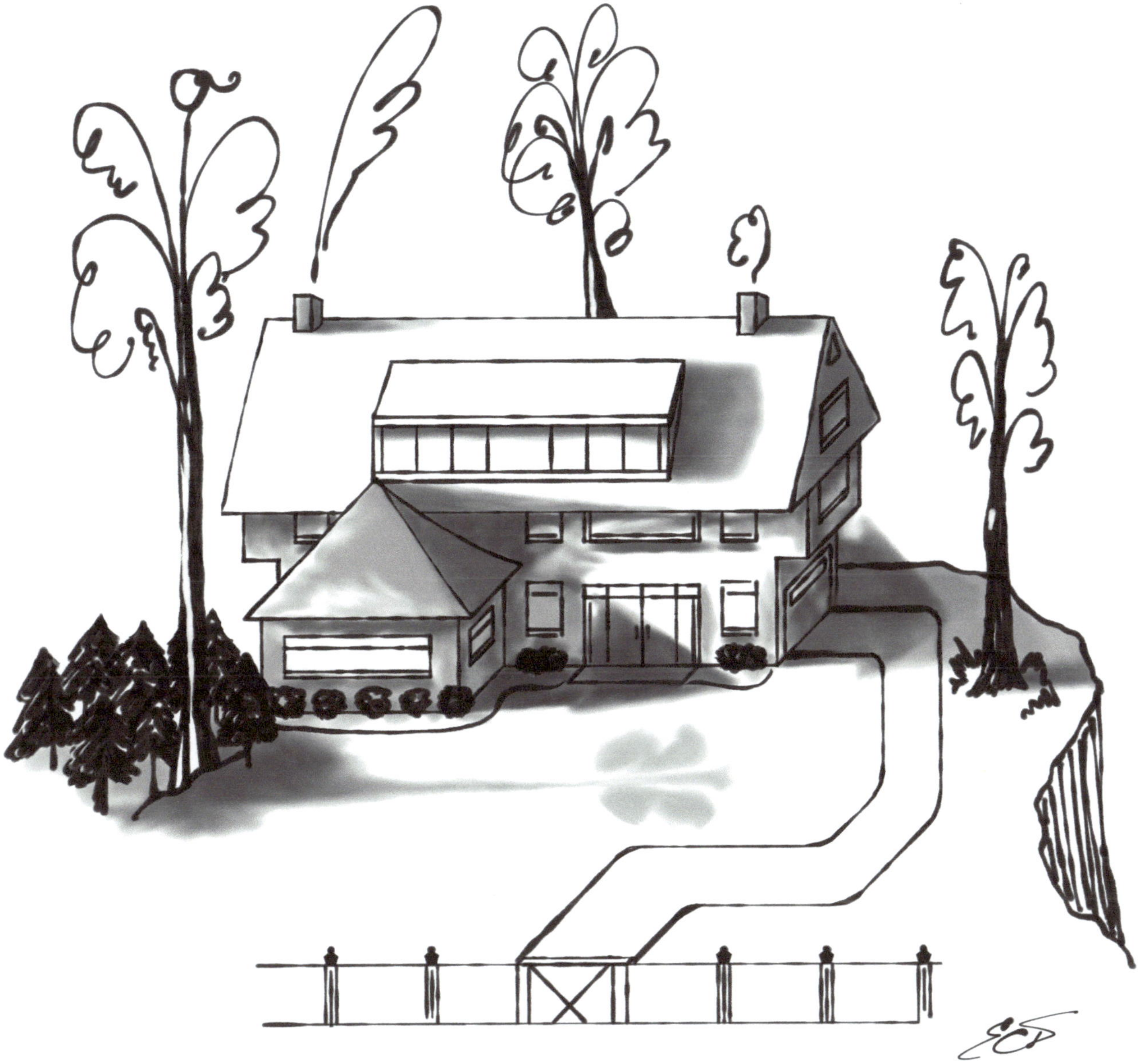

E. C. Flickinger
House on the Hill, 2017
Digital pen and ink

... especially the shadow of the 'butterfly tree.'"

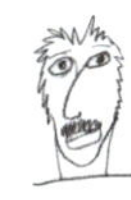

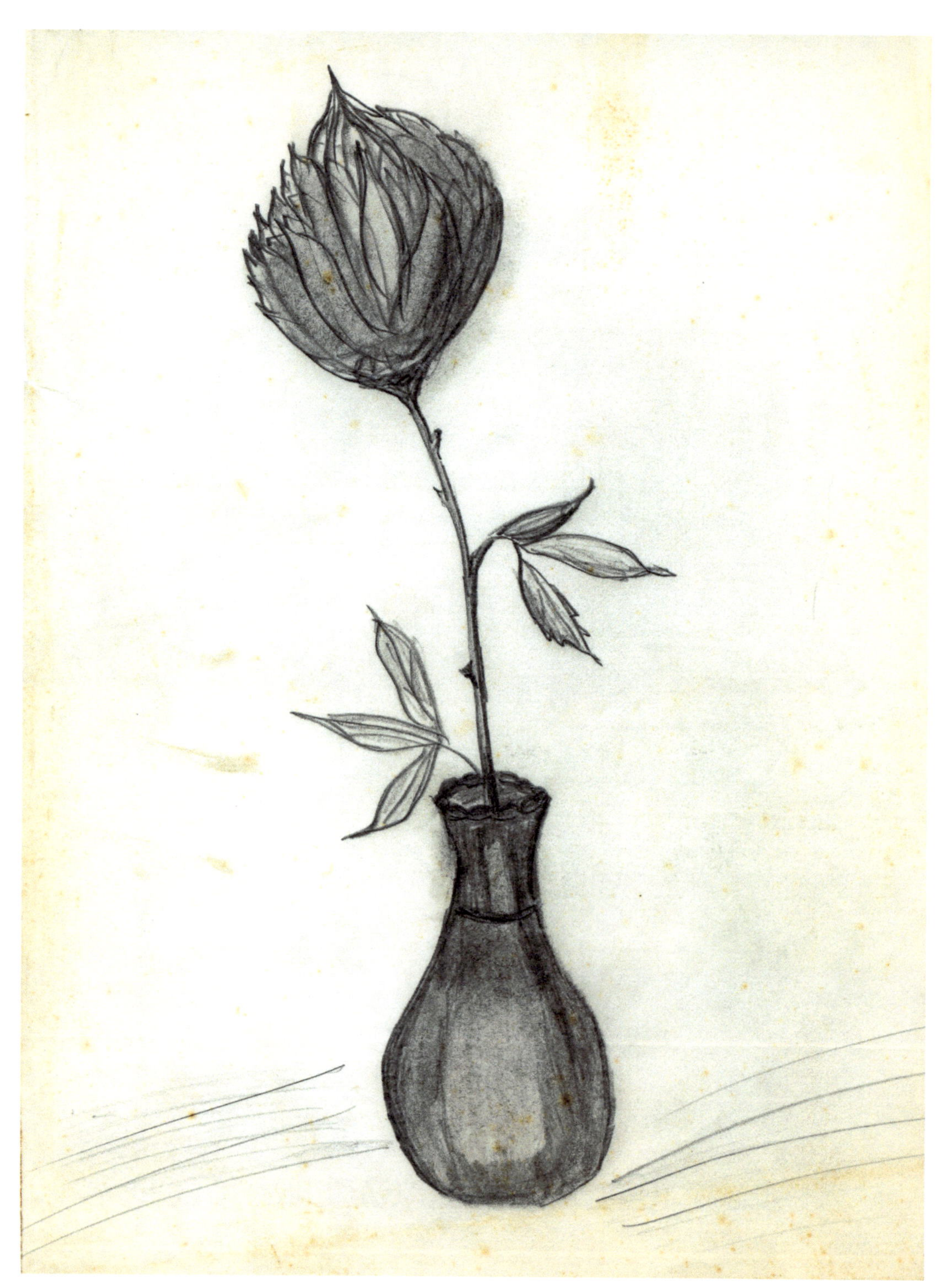

Paul H. Flickinger, Jr.
Single Flower in Vase
Pencil on paper
9 x 12 inches

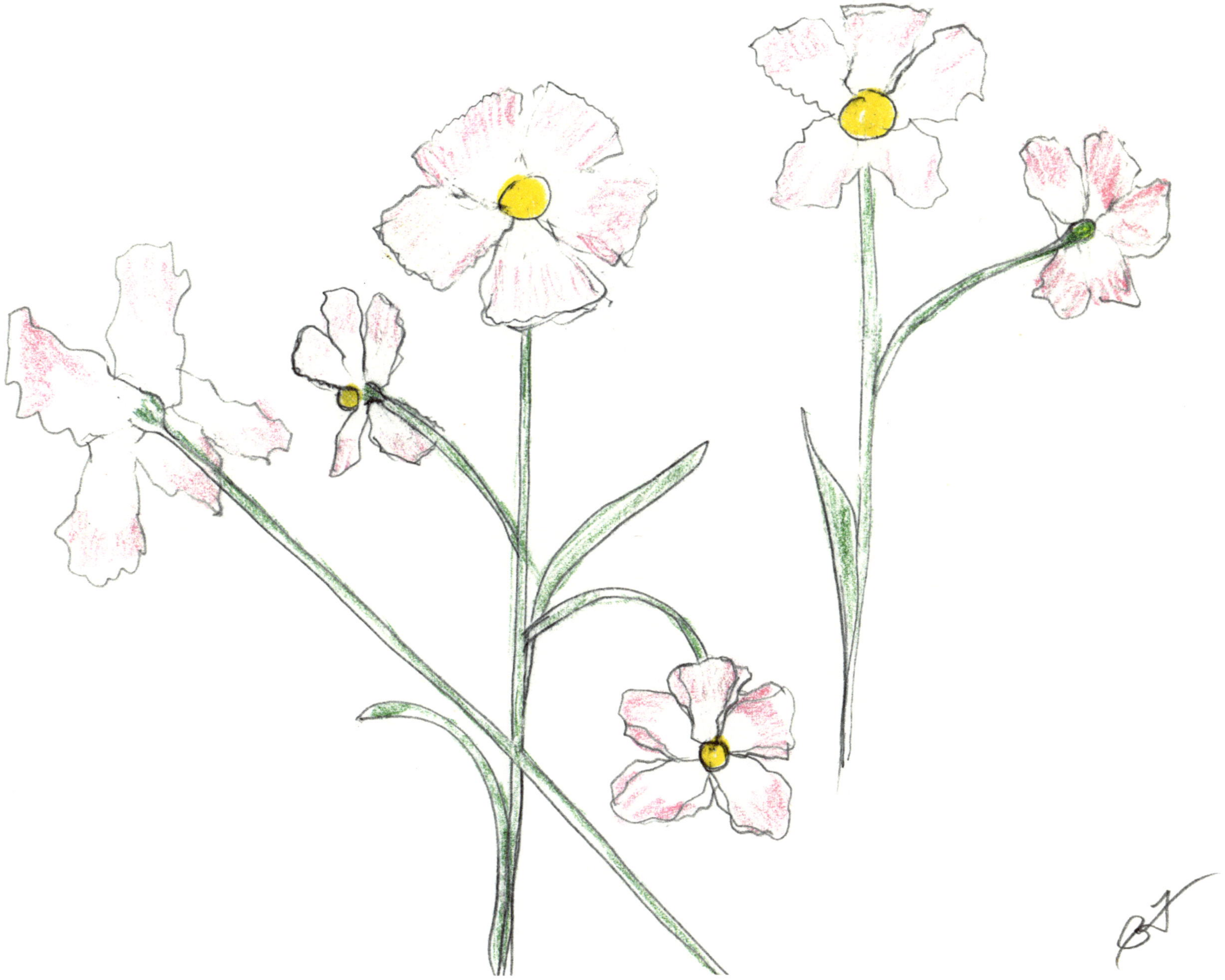

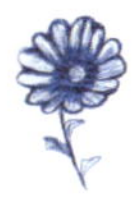

Paul H. Flickinger, Jr., *Pencil Flowers*
Pencil on paper, 12 x 9 inches

21

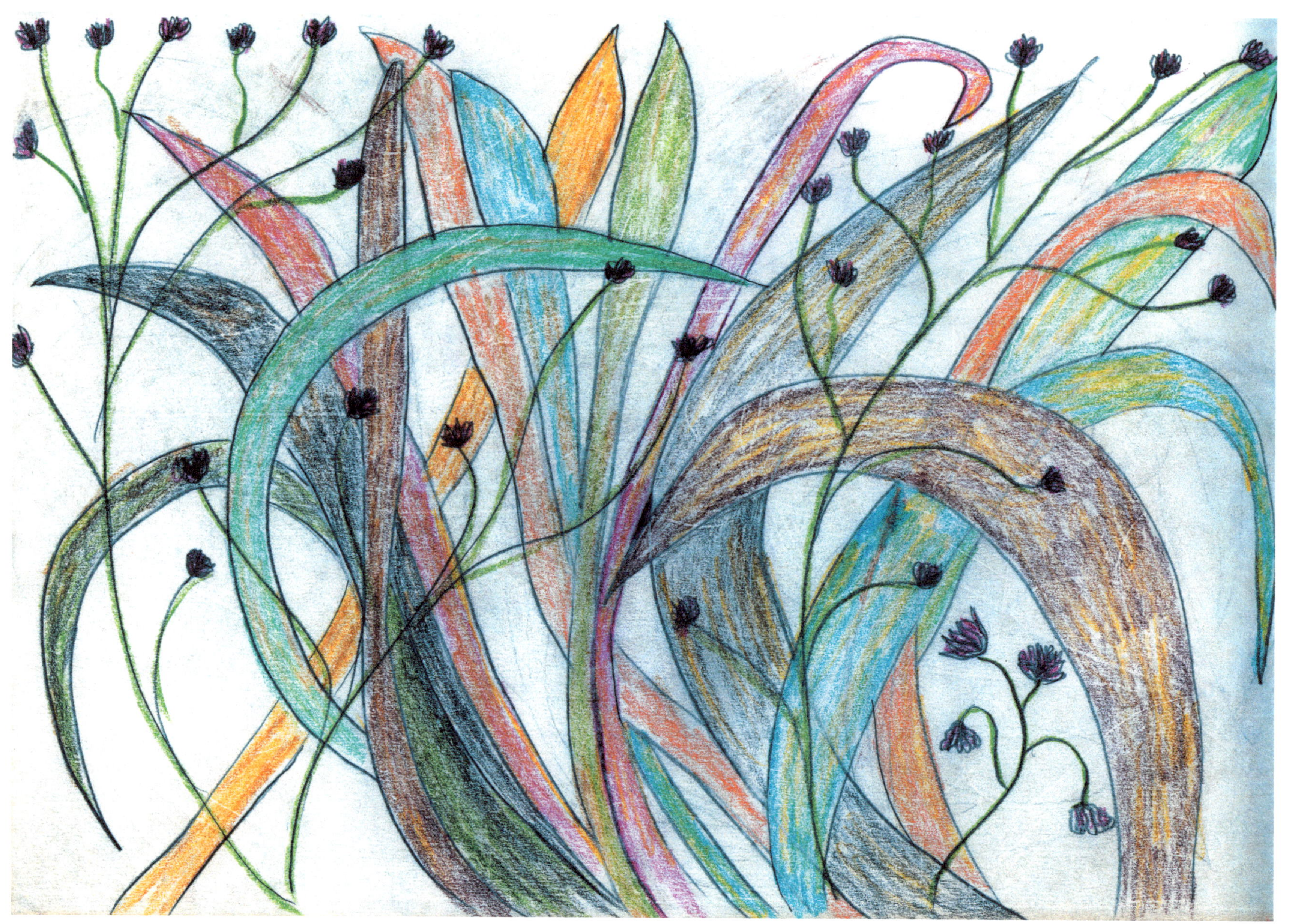

Paul H. Flickinger, Jr.
Breeze
Pencil on paper
18 x 12 inches

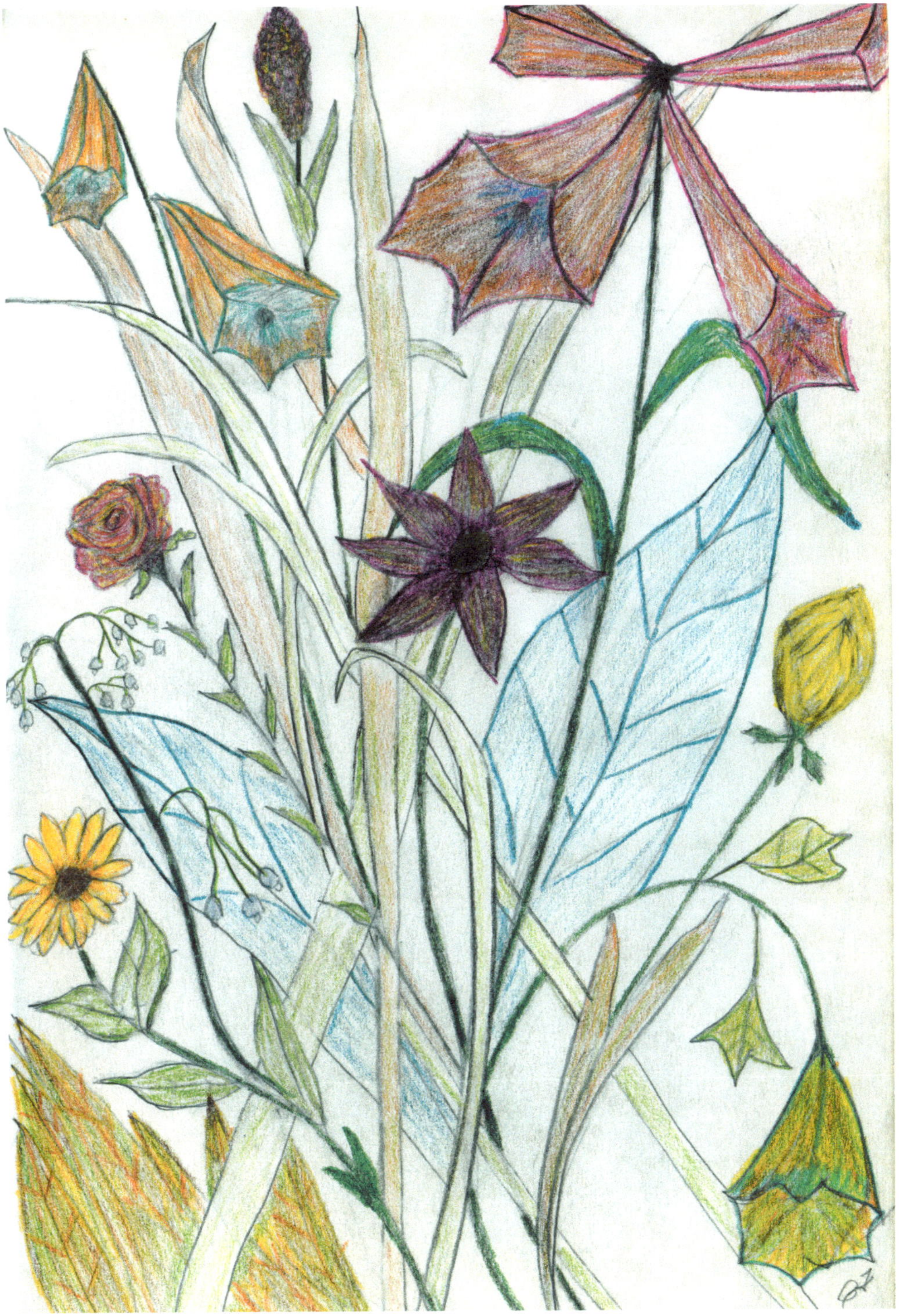

Paul H. Flickinger, Jr.
Pencil Garden
Pencil on paper
12 x 18 inches

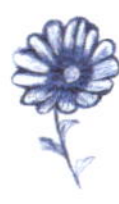

Paul

Paul H. Flickinger, Jr., the eldest child of Sarah and Paul, Sr., was born in February of 1936 in Pittsburgh, Pennsylvania.

Paul struggled as an adolescent until he spent a summer working on a farm. And on that farm, there were more than cows and chickens.

EI, EI, O.

On that farm, Paul found his strength, his purpose. That following fall, his test scores improved so dramatically that his teachers assumed he was cheating.

He soon proved them wrong by rising to the top of his class.

Paul and his high school sweetheart, Betty, married after graduation rather than attend college—a decision they never regretted.

Paul H. Flickinger, Jr.
Blue Trumpet, c. 1977
Acrylic on canvas
11 x 14 inches
Paul's first painting.

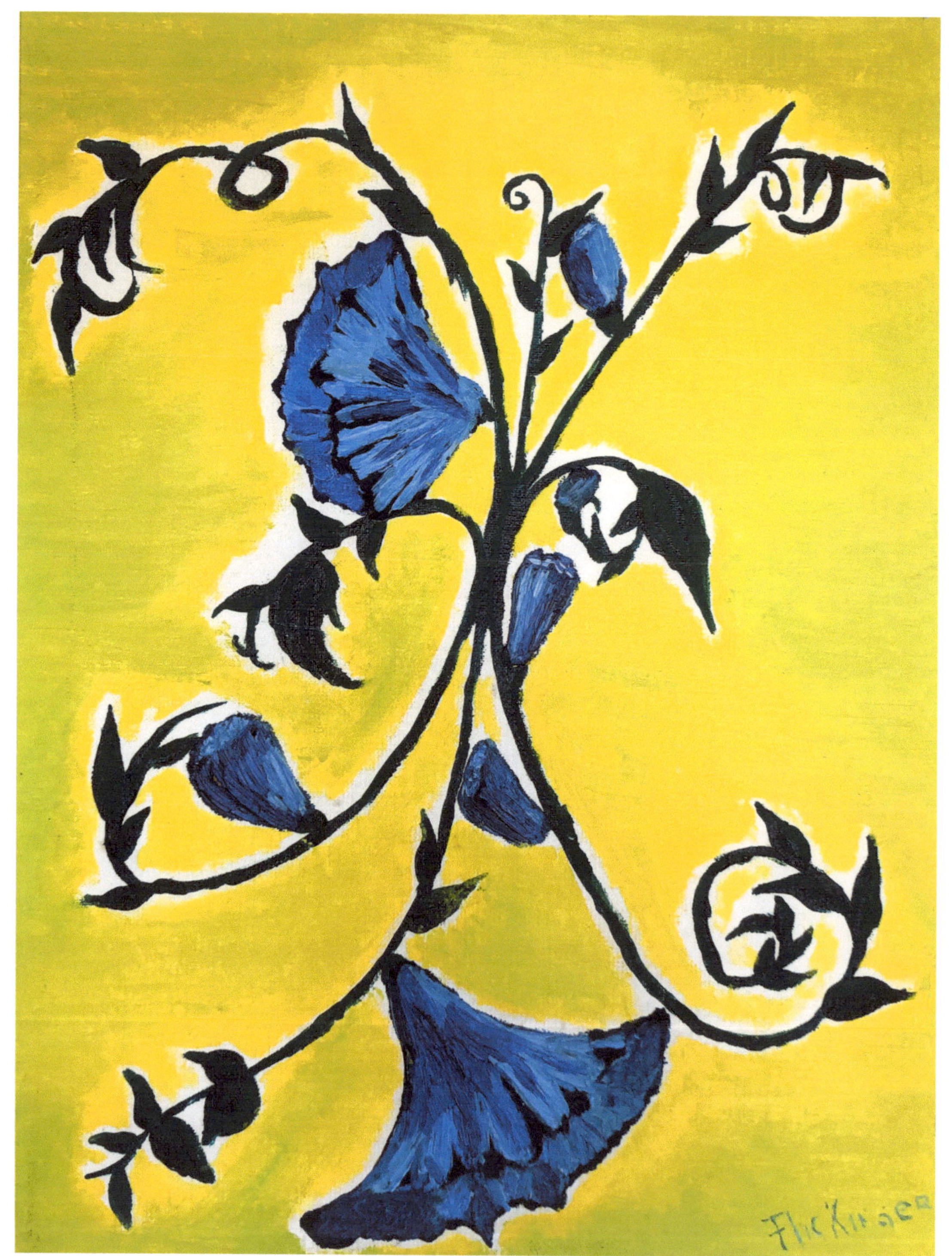

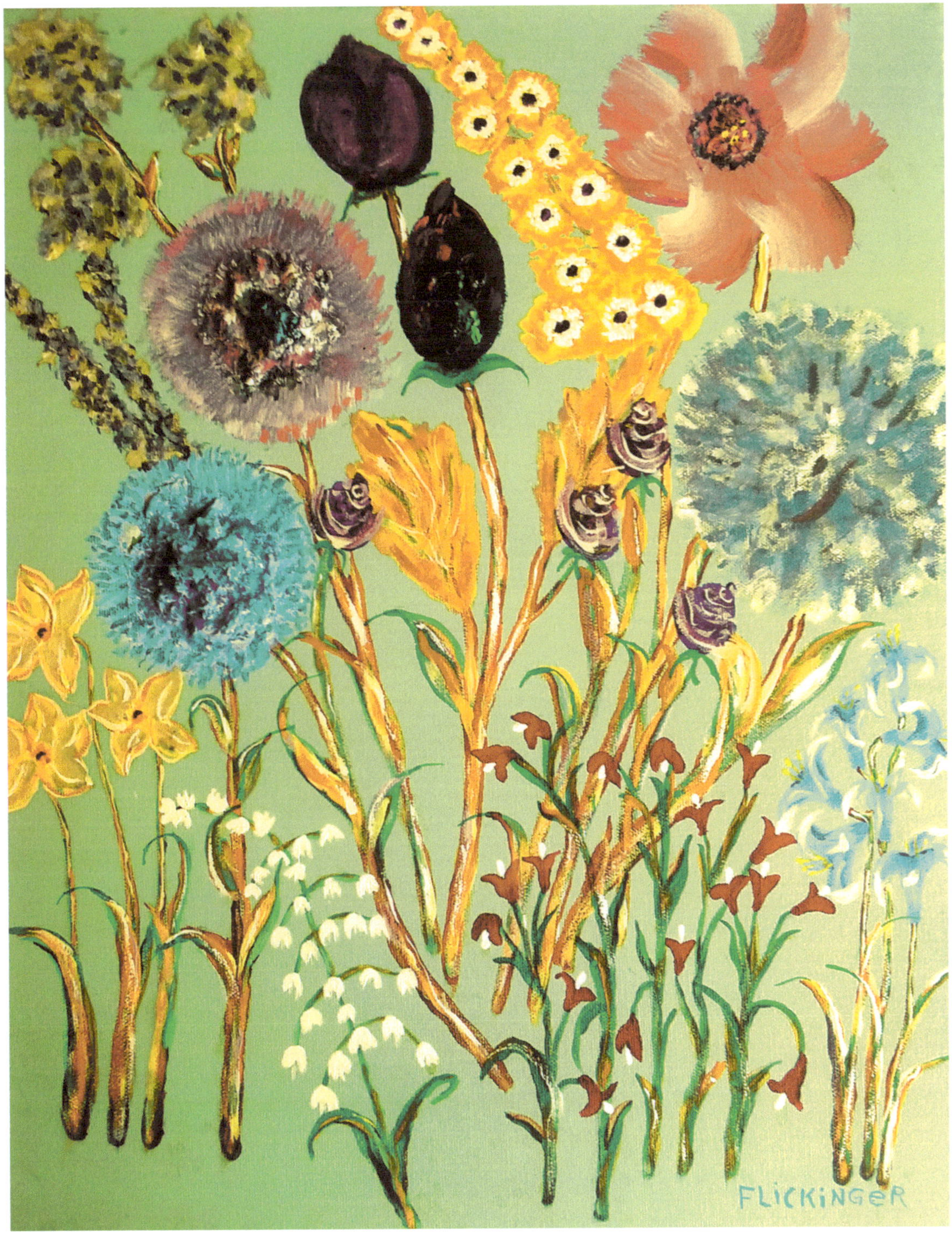

Paul and Betty brought five children into the world: William, Julia, Edward, Karen, and Richard.

"Things were simple growing up as a middle child," Edward shared. "I had two older siblings to learn from and when something went wrong, two younger siblings to blame.

"Unfortunately, simple can sometimes backfire, especially when a line is crossed. I don't remember what I did that afternoon, but I can still hear my mother warn me: 'wait till your father gets home.' Those six words were the most feared, especially when said in that order.

"I had to run very fast to avoid my father's belt, though he did give up after circling the dining room table for a mile or so.

"We were a family of good runners—and quick learners—there was no need to tempt fate."

Paul H. Flickinger, Jr.
Assorted Flowers
Acrylic on canvas
14 x 18 inches

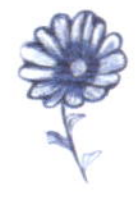

25

Paul wrote a lifetime of love songs, a heartful of poems to his wife.

Take My Hand

Take my hand, hold it tenderly,
Like the love deep in me,
Day by day.

Take my hand, hold it close,
Be with me
Day by day,
Year by year.

Take my hand, hold it tight.
Walk with me through this night.
Be it sad, be it bright.

Day by day.

Year by year.

And forever more true.

–Paul

Paul H. Flickinger, Jr.
A Golden Life, c. 1979
Acrylic on canvas
12 x 16 inches

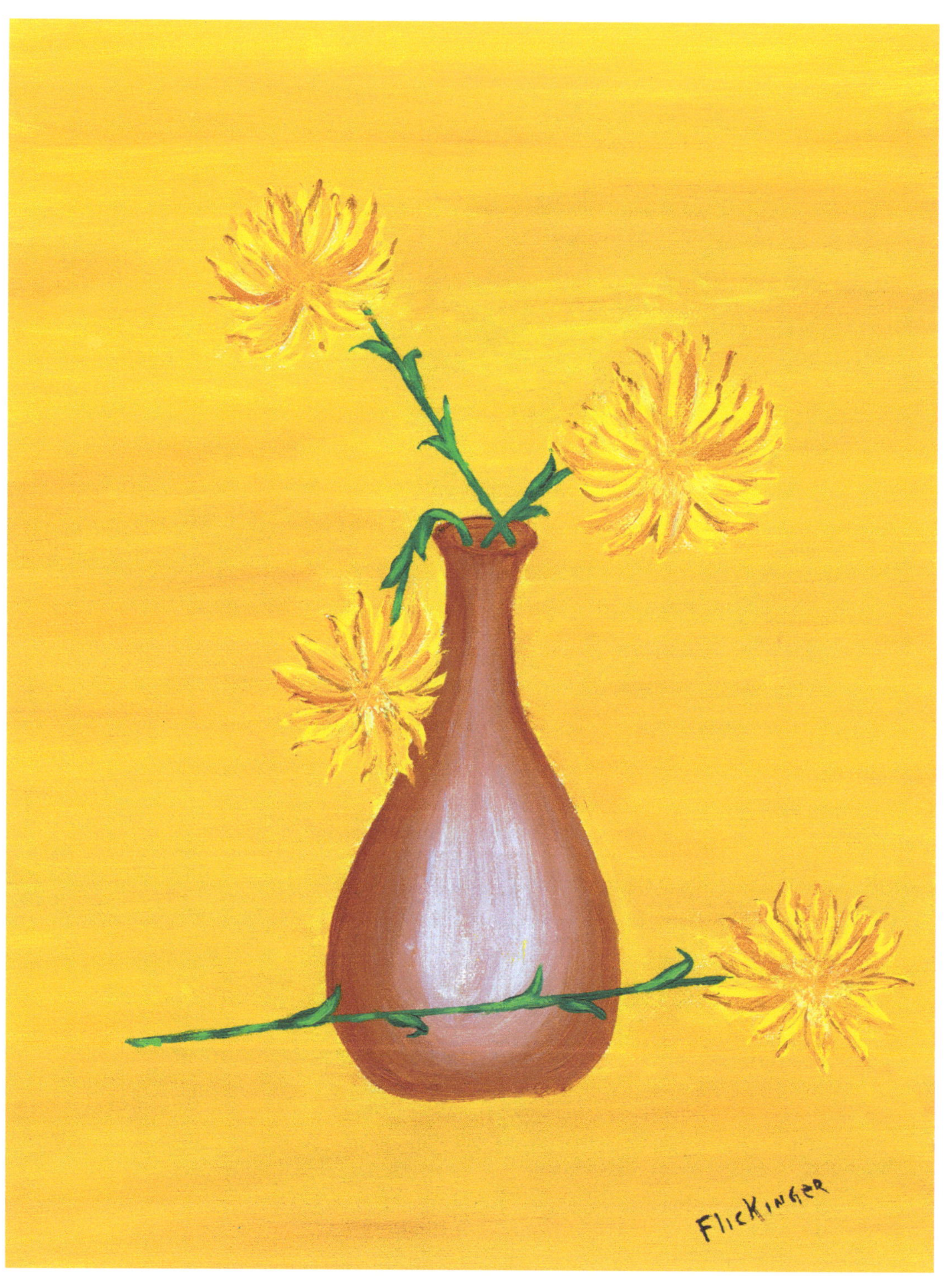

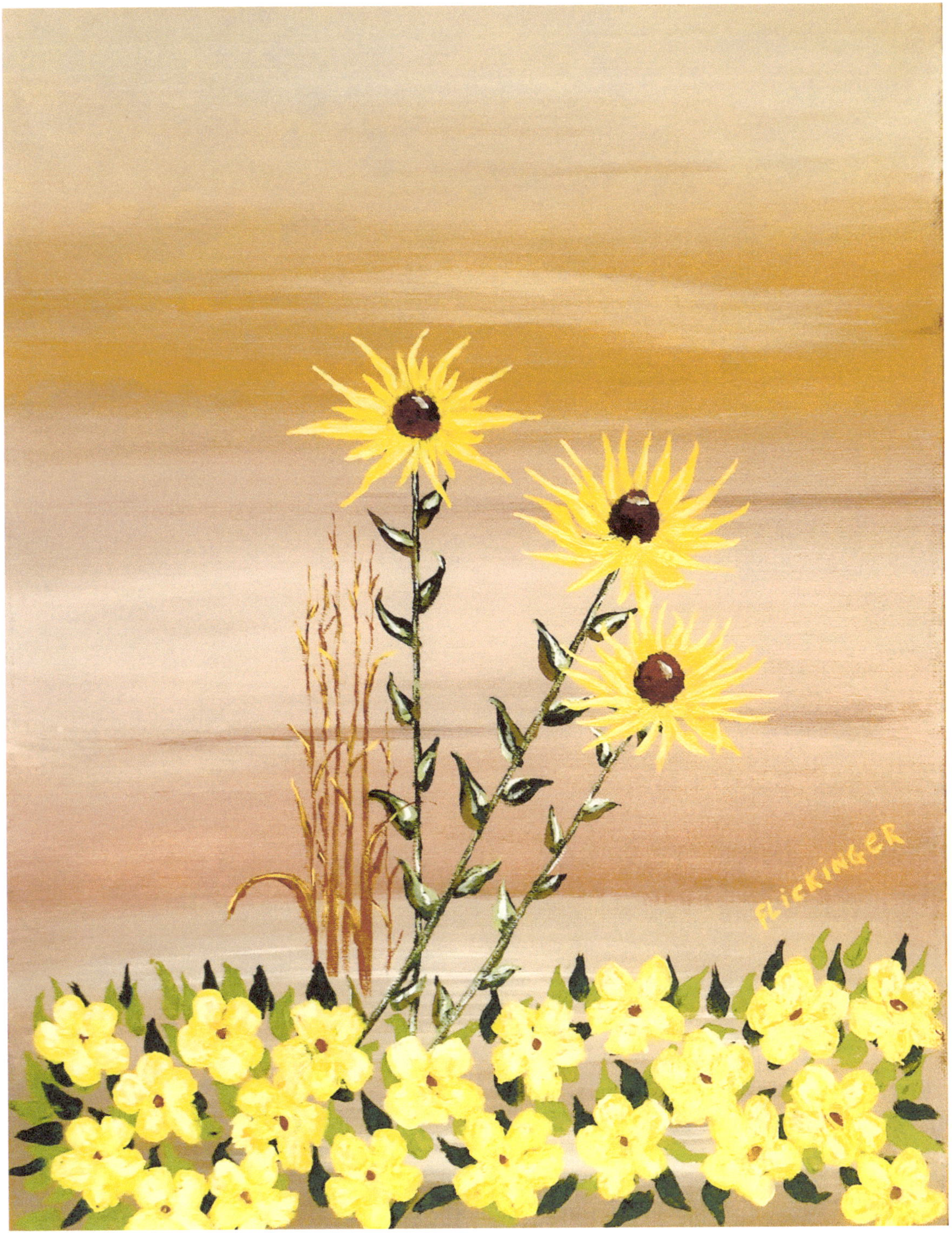

In October of 1996, Paul wrote these lyrics to sing to his then thirty-something daughters.

You're Still My Little Girl

You're still my little girl,
and always will be.

No matter how the years pass,
you always will be.

You'll never grow up in my heart,
For there you are still a part.

You're still my little girl,
and always will be.

No matter how the years pass,
you will always be

My little girl to me.

–Dad

Paul H. Flickinger, Jr.
Assorted Flowers
Acrylic on canvas
14 x 18 inches

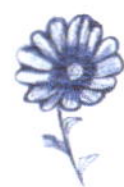

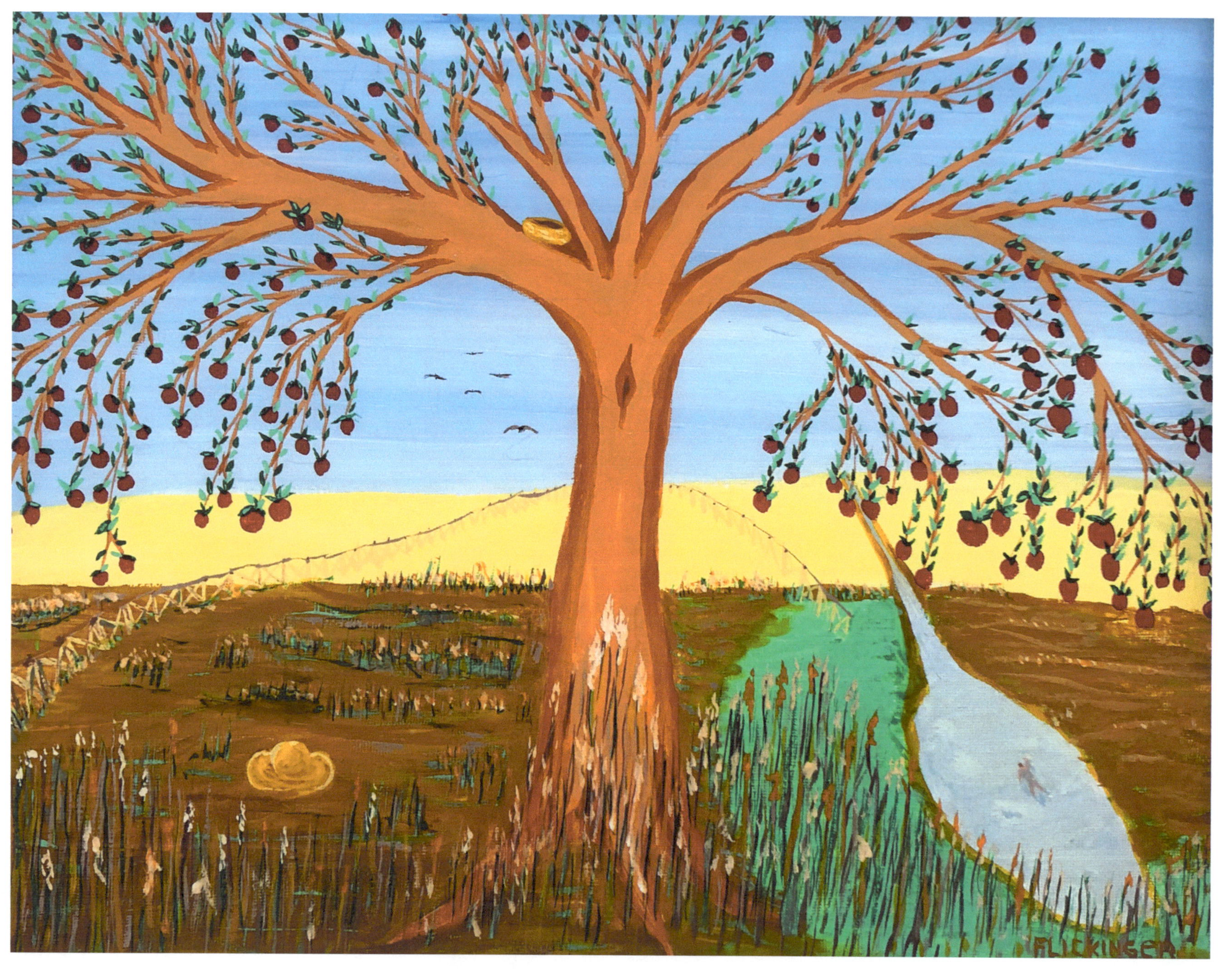

Paul H. Flickinger, Jr., *Under the Apple Tree*
Acrylic on canvas, 16 x 12 inches

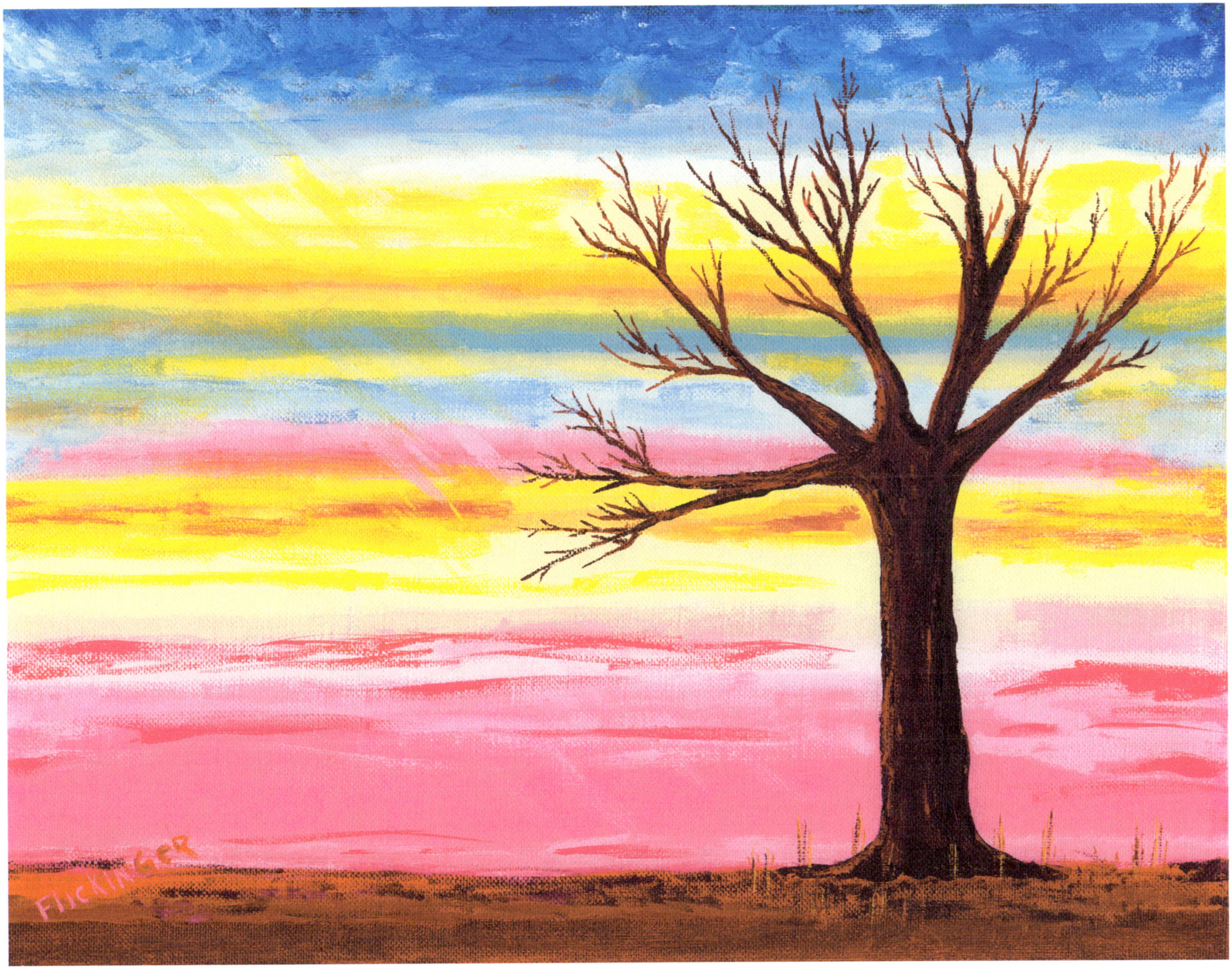

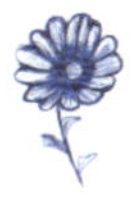

Paul H. Flickinger, Jr., *Rainbow Sky*, c. 1978
Acrylic on canvas, 16 x 12 inches

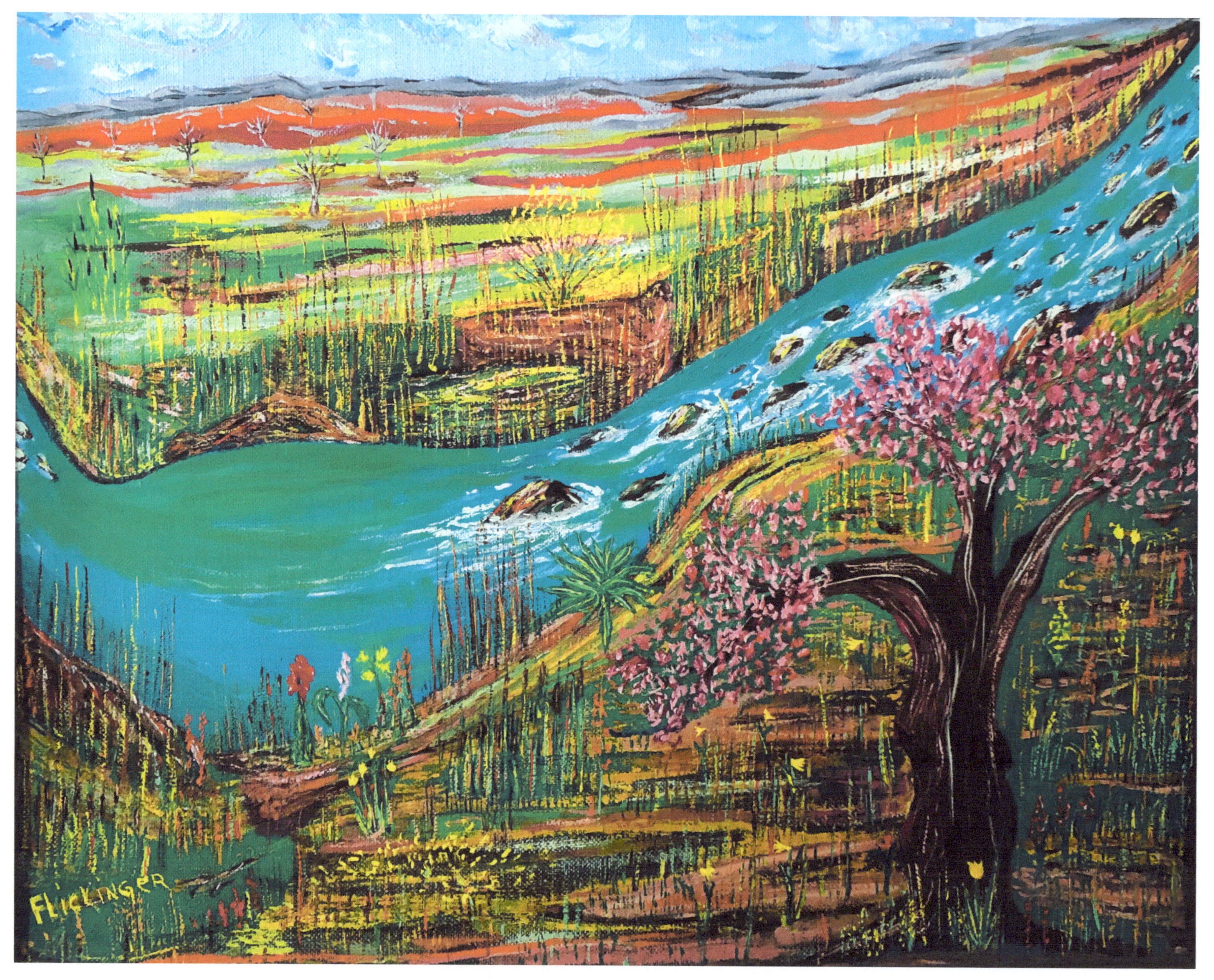

Paul H. Flickinger, Jr., *River Bend*
Acrylic on canvas, 18 x 14 inches

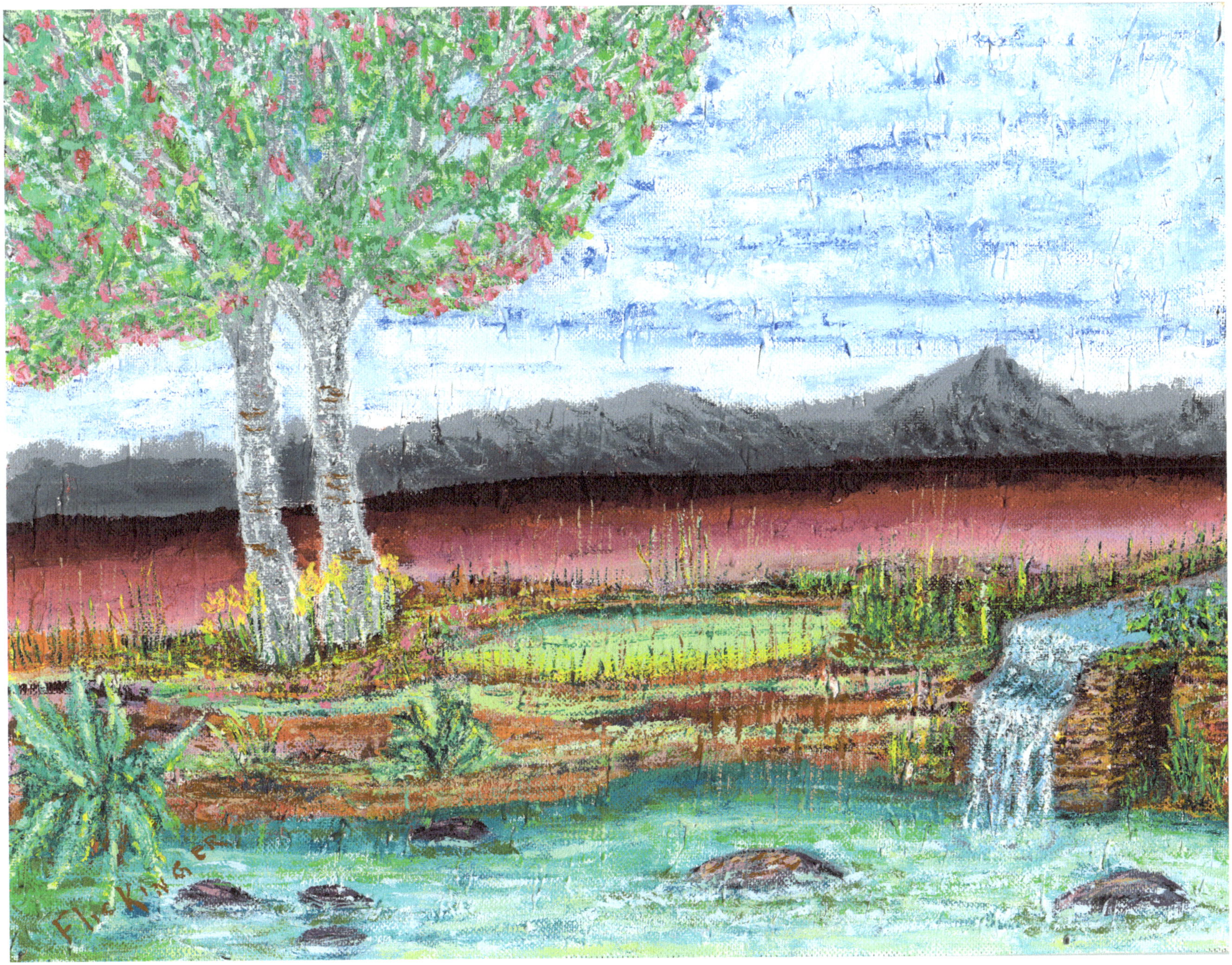

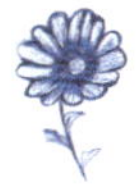

Paul H. Flickinger, Jr., *Oasis*
Acrylic on canvas, 16 x 12 inches

Paul will be missed.

Paul died of cancer only two years into retirement, but not before cleaning every drawer, every closet—and not before painting this gem, his masterpiece.

The world lost a great artist on that day in December, 2003.

His wife lost the love of her life.

His five children lost their dad.

This painting hangs proudly in the home of Paul's son, Richard Flickinger.

"He was always the favorite"—a gift often bestowed upon the baby of a family.

Paul H. Flickinger, Jr.
Sunset on the Beach
Acrylic on canvas
10 x 14 inches

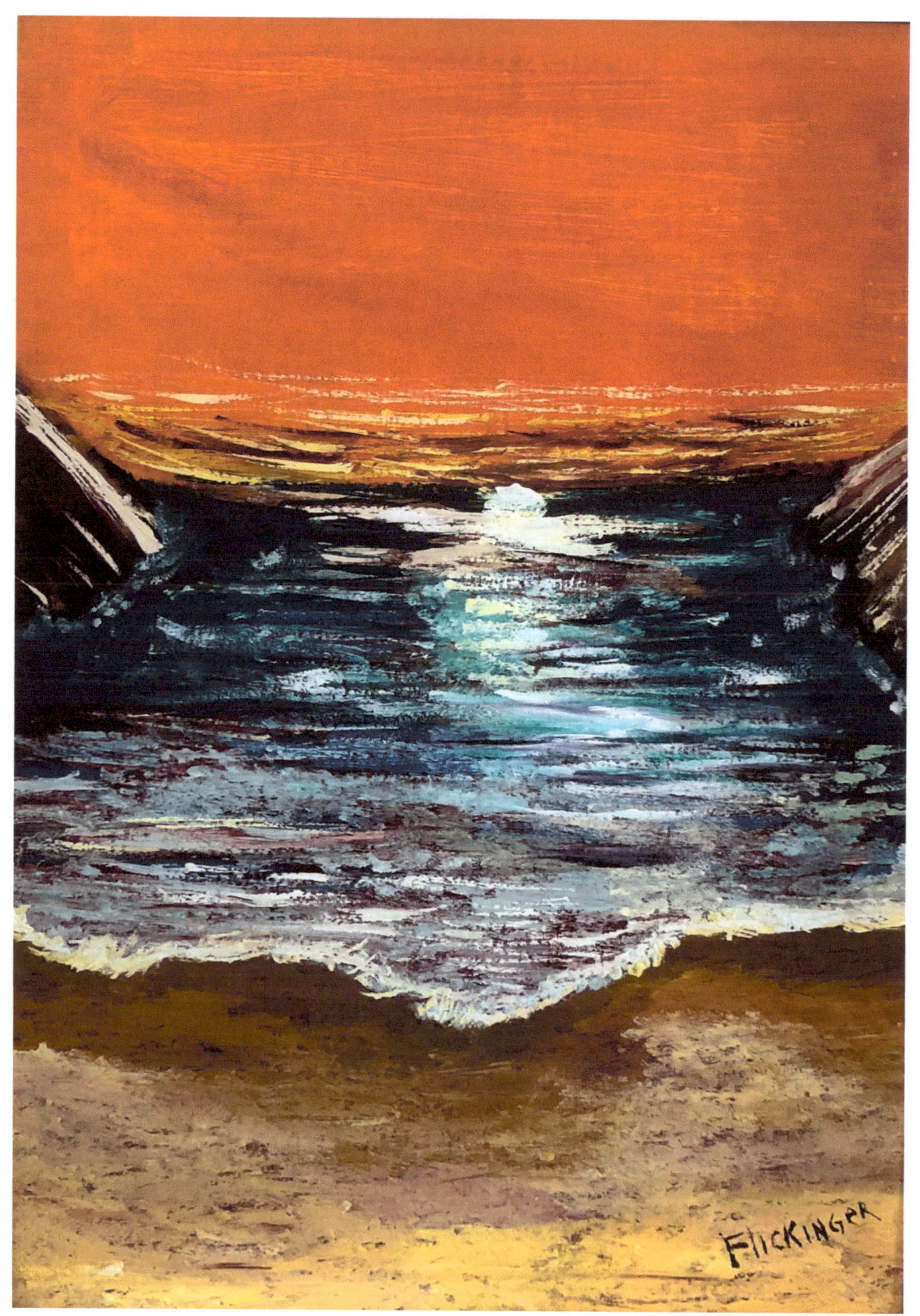

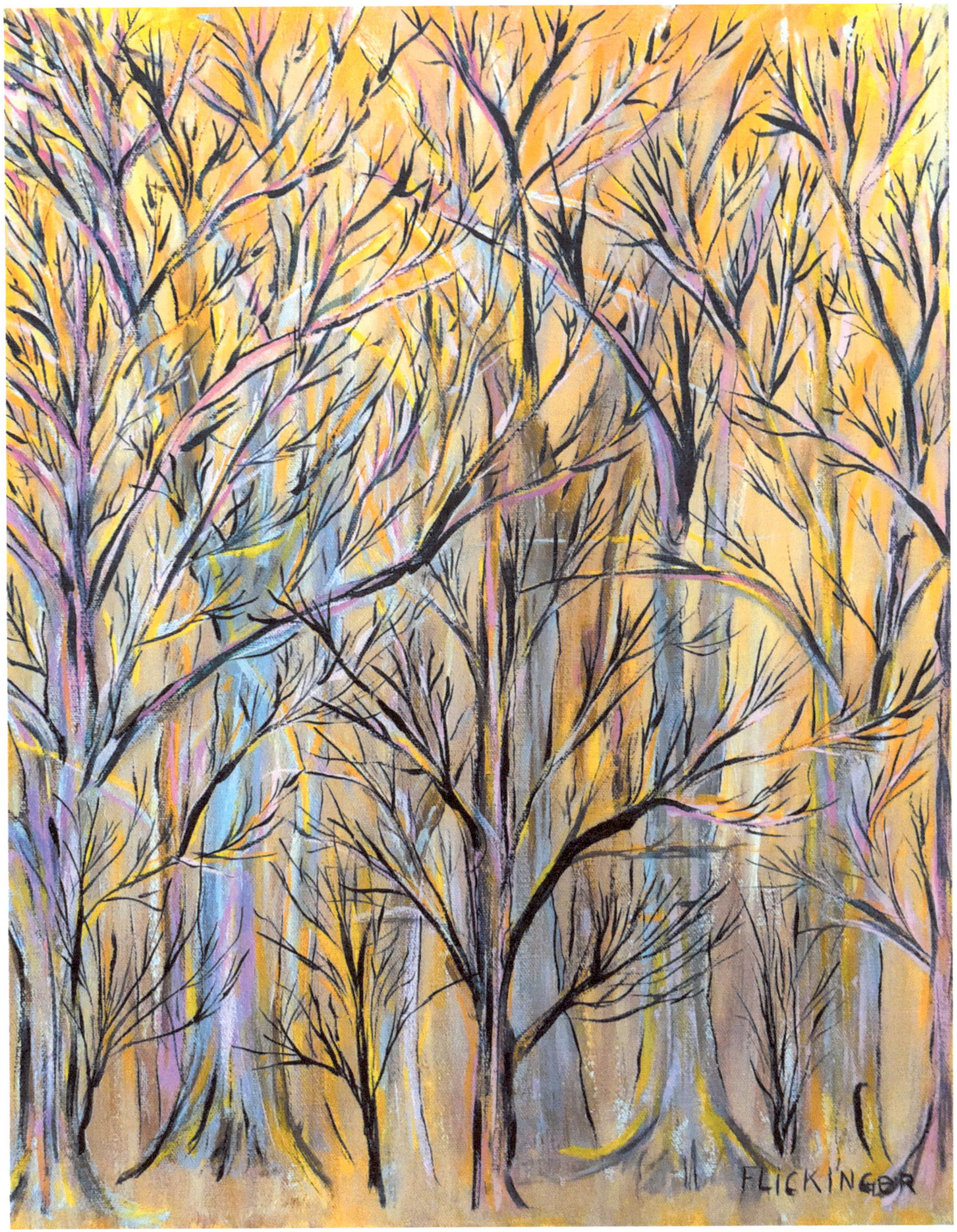

Encore!

Paul was a son, a husband, a father, a grandfather, and a self-taught artist. He passed before the birth of his first great grandchild.

Paul loved his family.

Paul loved to paint.

This painting hangs proudly in the home of Paul's granddaughter, Sarah Wimberley.

Paul H. Flickinger, Jr.
Trees of the Forest
Acrylic on canvas
16 x 20 inches

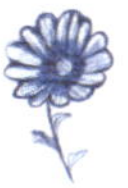

33

Edward

Edward Charles Flickinger was born in 1960 in a small town in Western Pennsylvania.

He earned a Bachelor of Science degree in Computer Science from The Pennsylvania State University and a Graduate Certificate in Project Management from The George Washington University. He co-invented two U.S. patents.

After a thirty-three career in software development, he retired to a life of writing, painting, and grand-parenting.

Edward has authored one novel and a book of poetry. A novella trilogy is in the works.

The father of two children, Sarah and James, Edward currently lives with his wife, Wendy, in a small town in Eastern Pennsylvania.

Pencil sketches were his first love.

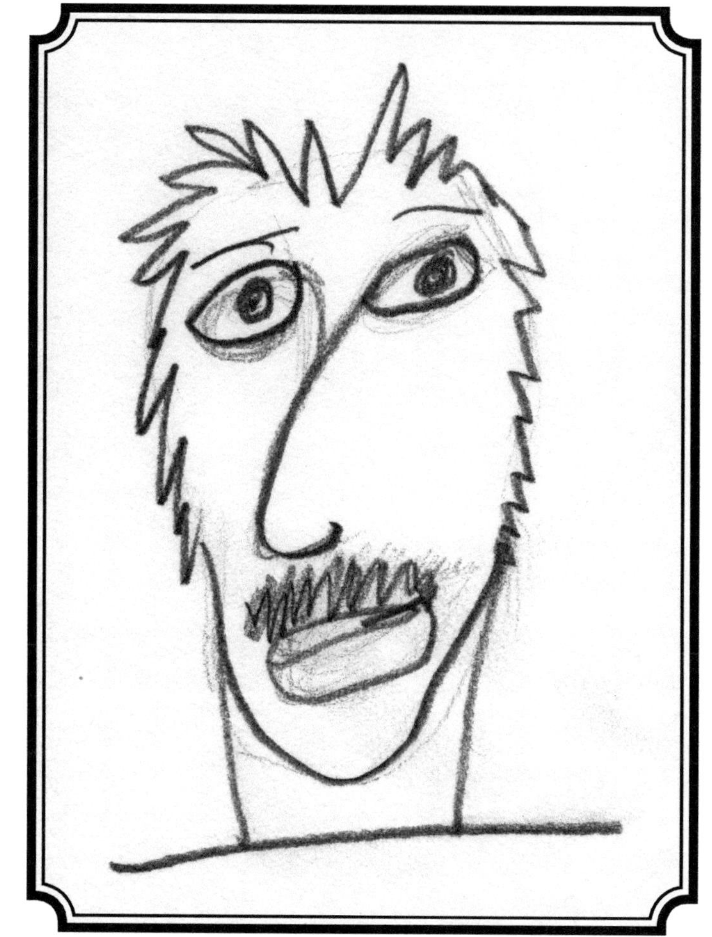

E. C. Flickinger
Self-portrait, c. 1995
Pencil on paper
3.5 x 5 inches

"Well technically, my second; I had an awful crush on a second-grade classmate. Still, there is something fundamentally pure about drawing in pencil."

At the age of seven, Edward earned a summer of Tam O'Shanter art classes at the Carnegie Hall of Music with his submission of an adult bird walking a young bird on a leash.

"I remember the first time we climbed the stairs of the Carnegie Hall of Music. My father stopped before the three archways. His face was intense, full of admiration. I asked him which path we should take. He told me it didn't matter. Any child could enter through any door he or she wished.

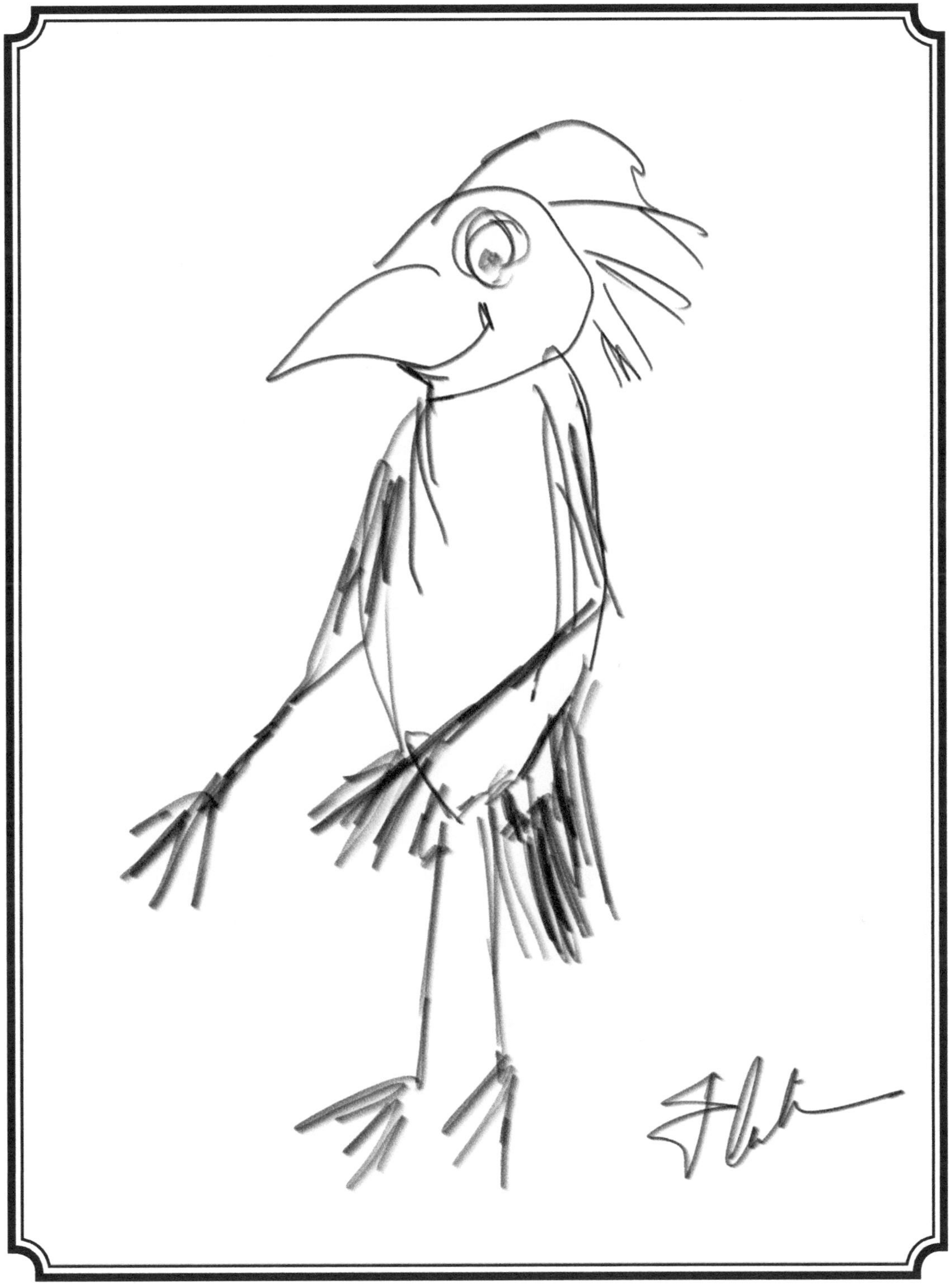

"I smiled and picked the center archway; my dad did too. Once inside, there was shouting, lots of shouting: 'Girls to the left, boys to the right.' I had no idea art was so structured, so serious, but I did learn some valuable drawing techniques that summer, including two-point perspective.

"My submission wasn't the least bit special until I added the smaller bird and drew in the leash. Back in April of 1968, no one even considered harnessing a child, so the piece took on an air of social commentary. 'Was the smaller bird really younger? Was that poor bird controlled—owned?—by an oppressive society?'"

Edward laughed. "Look, I was seven and the drawing was due that day. I didn't have time to draw a dog."

Although that infamous sketch did not survive the fifty plus years since its creation, the bird character itself, Finch, still lives on today.

E. C. Flickinger
Finch
Digital spray paint

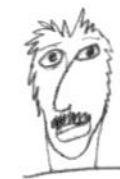

Paul

(1936 - 2003)

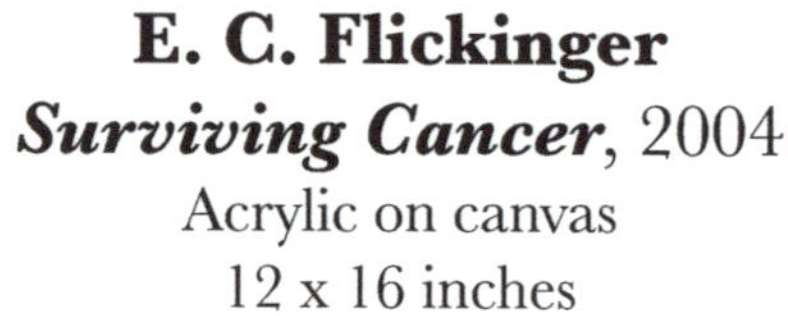

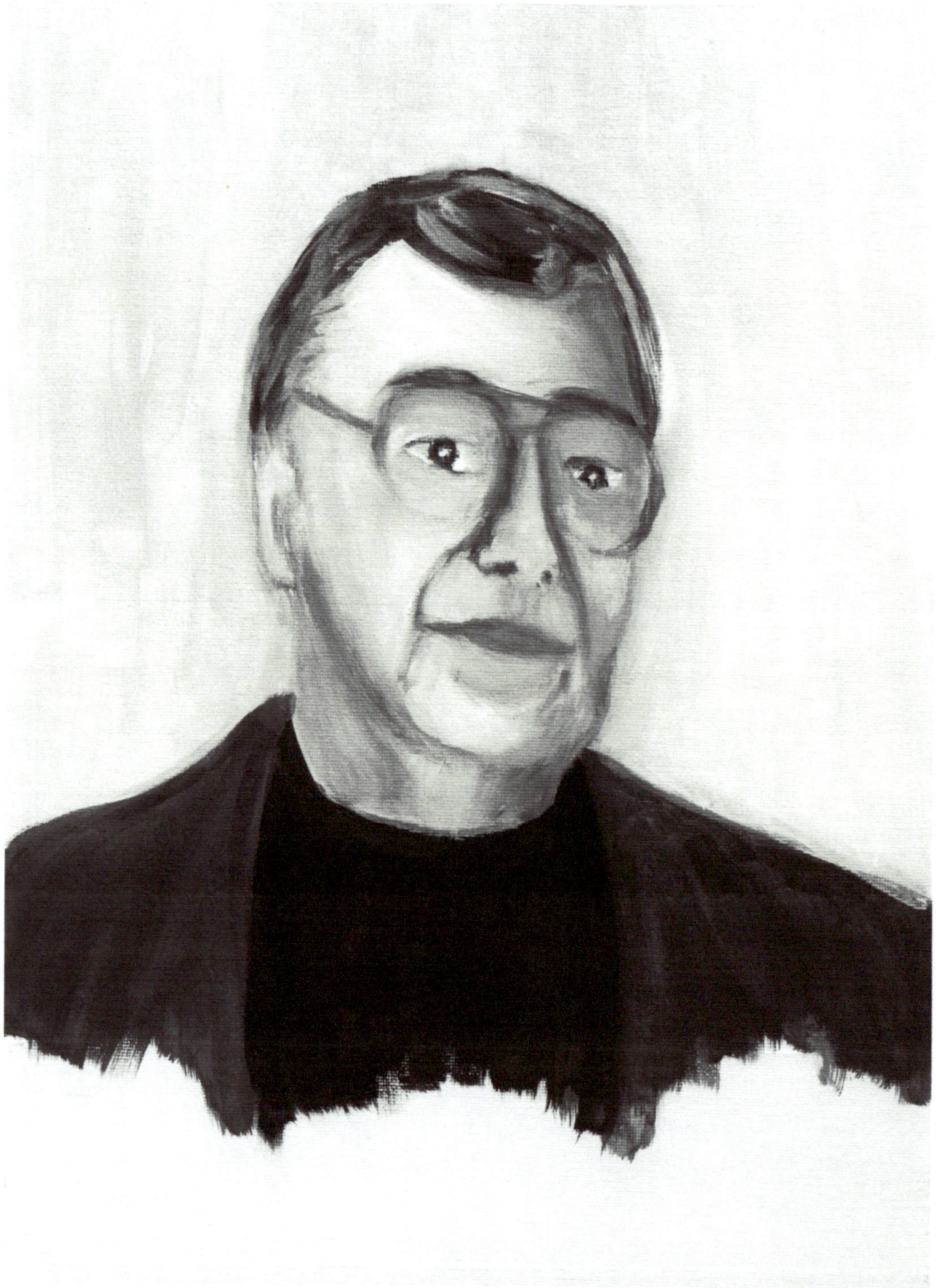

E. C. Flickinger
Surviving Cancer, 2004
Acrylic on canvas
12 x 16 inches

TCB

(1926 - 2009)

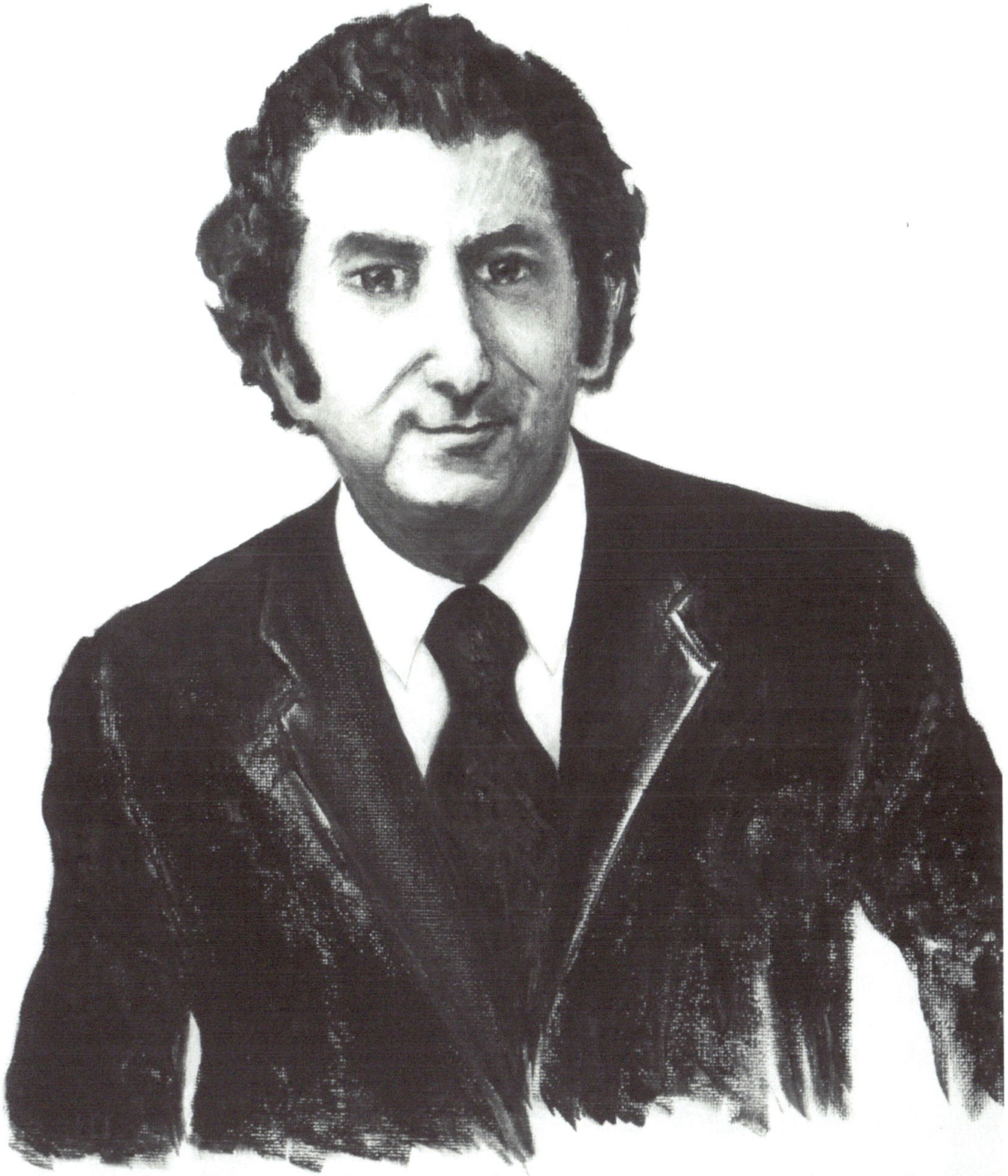

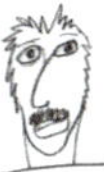

E. C. Flickinger
TCB, 2009
Acrylic on canvas
12 x 16 inches

Wendy

Wendy is featured in *Adam's Journal: A Novel* by E. C. Flickinger.

"Draw a picture of your next girlfriend. Take your time with it—think carefully about what she's doing right now; think long and hard about the lines of her face. Oh, but don't finish the drawing—leave a few stray lines on it to symbolize that she won't be complete until she meets you. You both are looking for each other."

"Wow."

"Get going; summer is almost over. Think—what is she doing now?"

"She's dreaming. She's waiting for me like I'm waiting for her."

—From *Adam's Journal,*
a dialogue between Sam and Adam

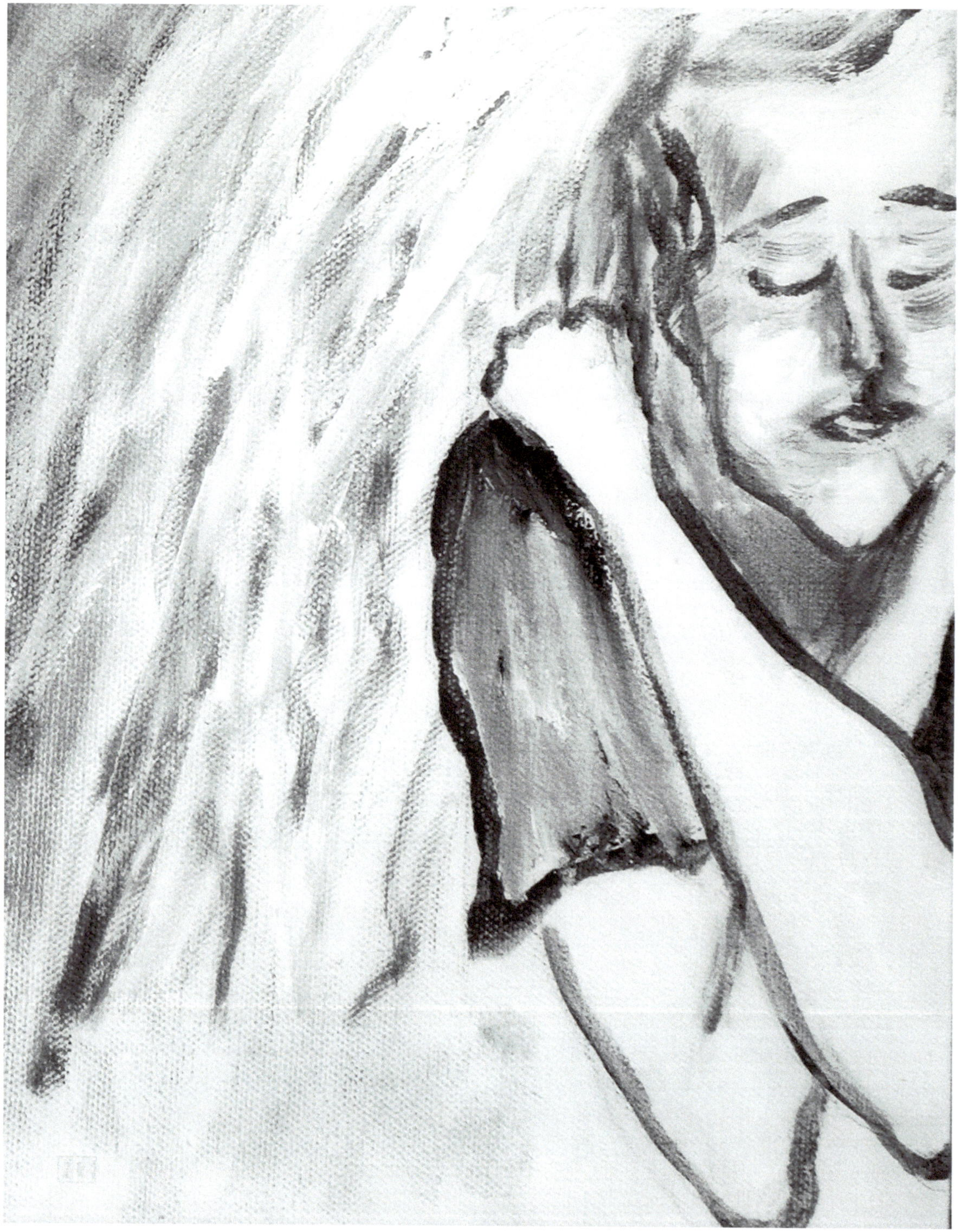

E. C. Flickinger
Wendy, 2016
Acrylic on canvas
8 x 10 inches

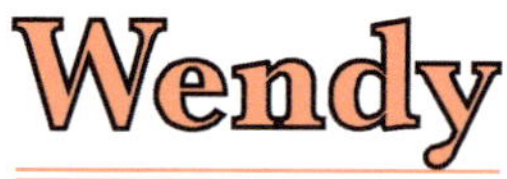

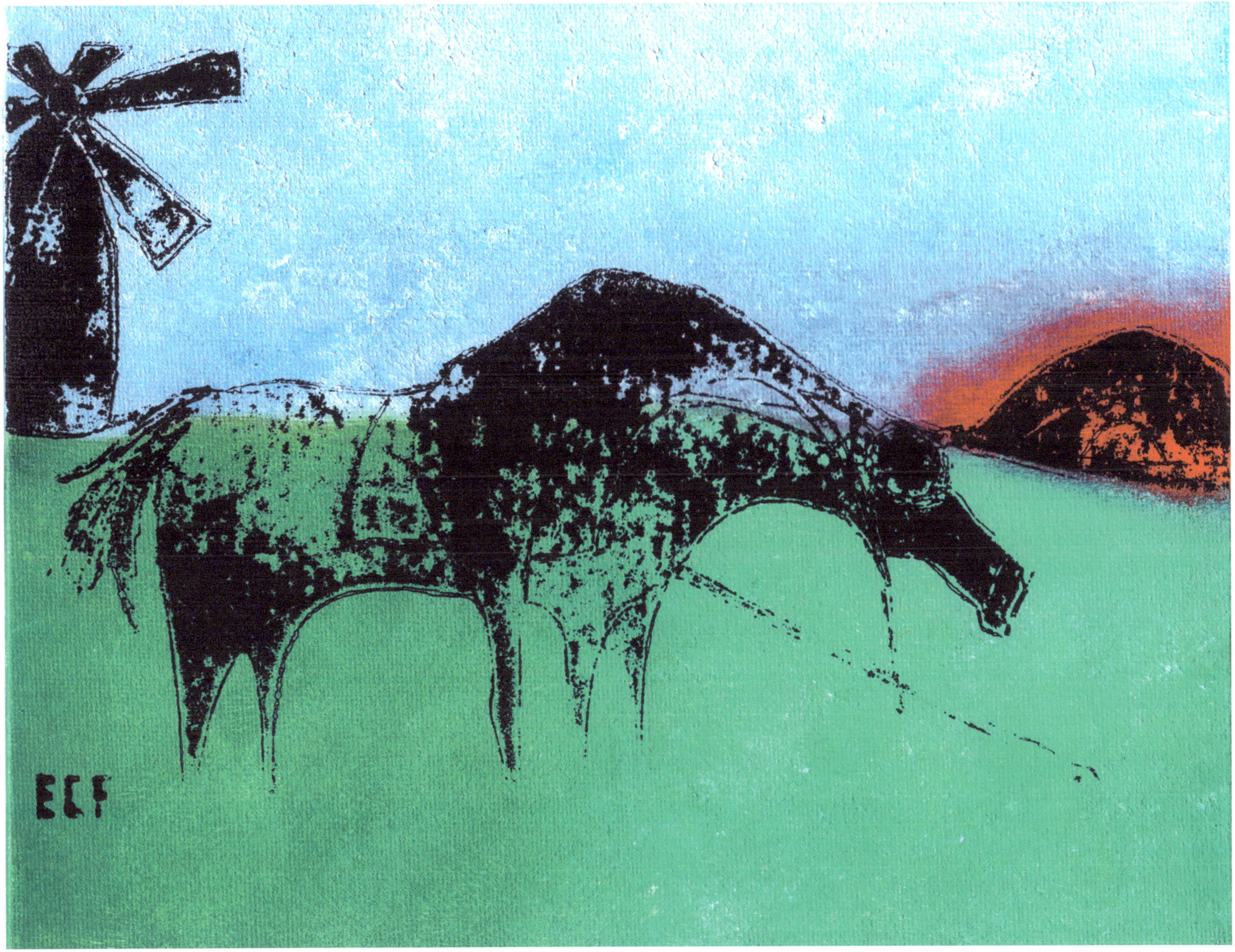

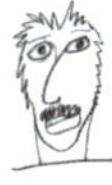

E. C. Flickinger, *Live To Fight Another Day*, 2007
Mixed media (block print overlaying acrylic on canvas), 10 x 8 inches

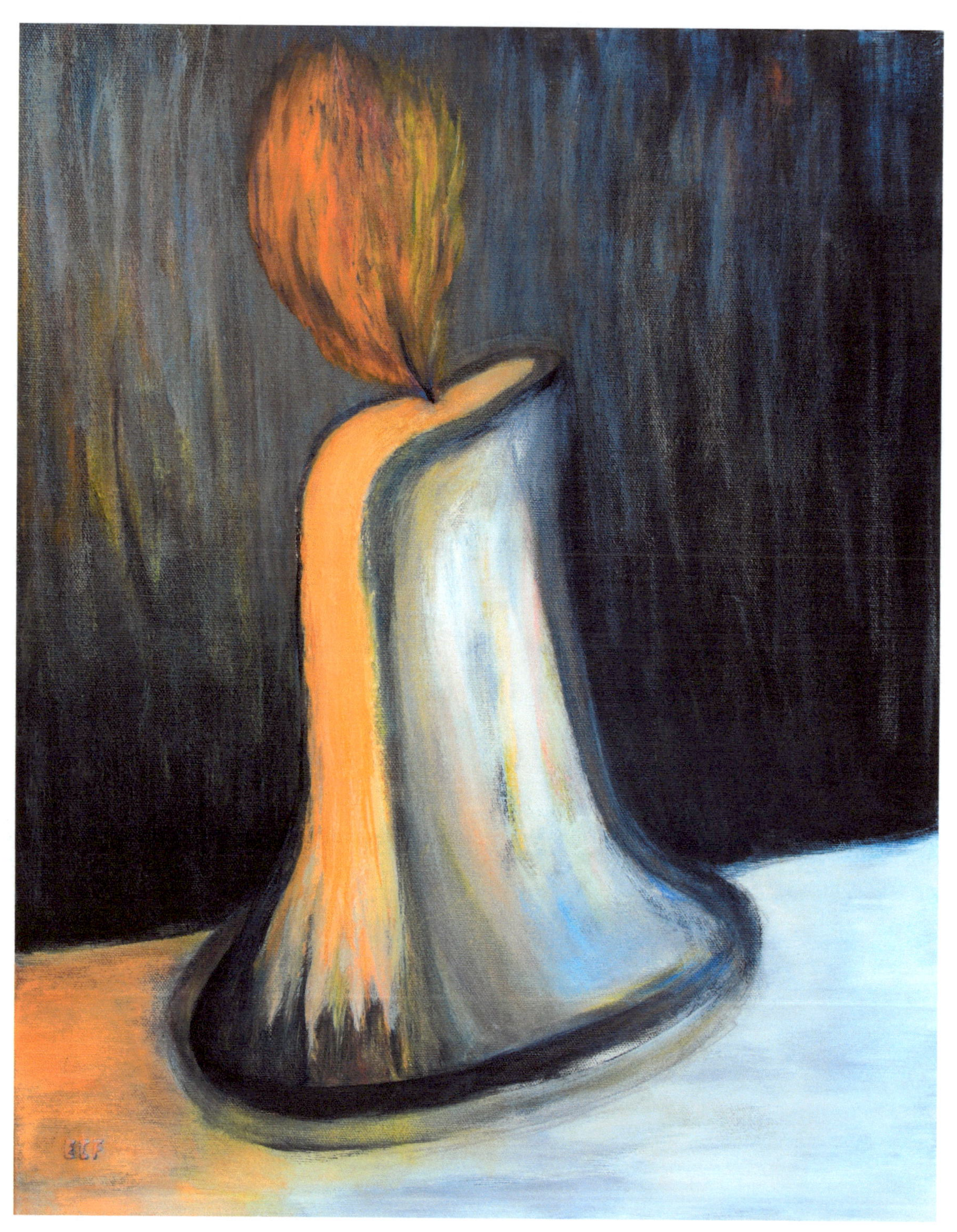

Die Kerze

Inspired by Dieter Kreig

E. C. Flickinger
***Die Kerze (The Candle)**, 2008*
Acrylic on canvas
16 x 20 inches

40

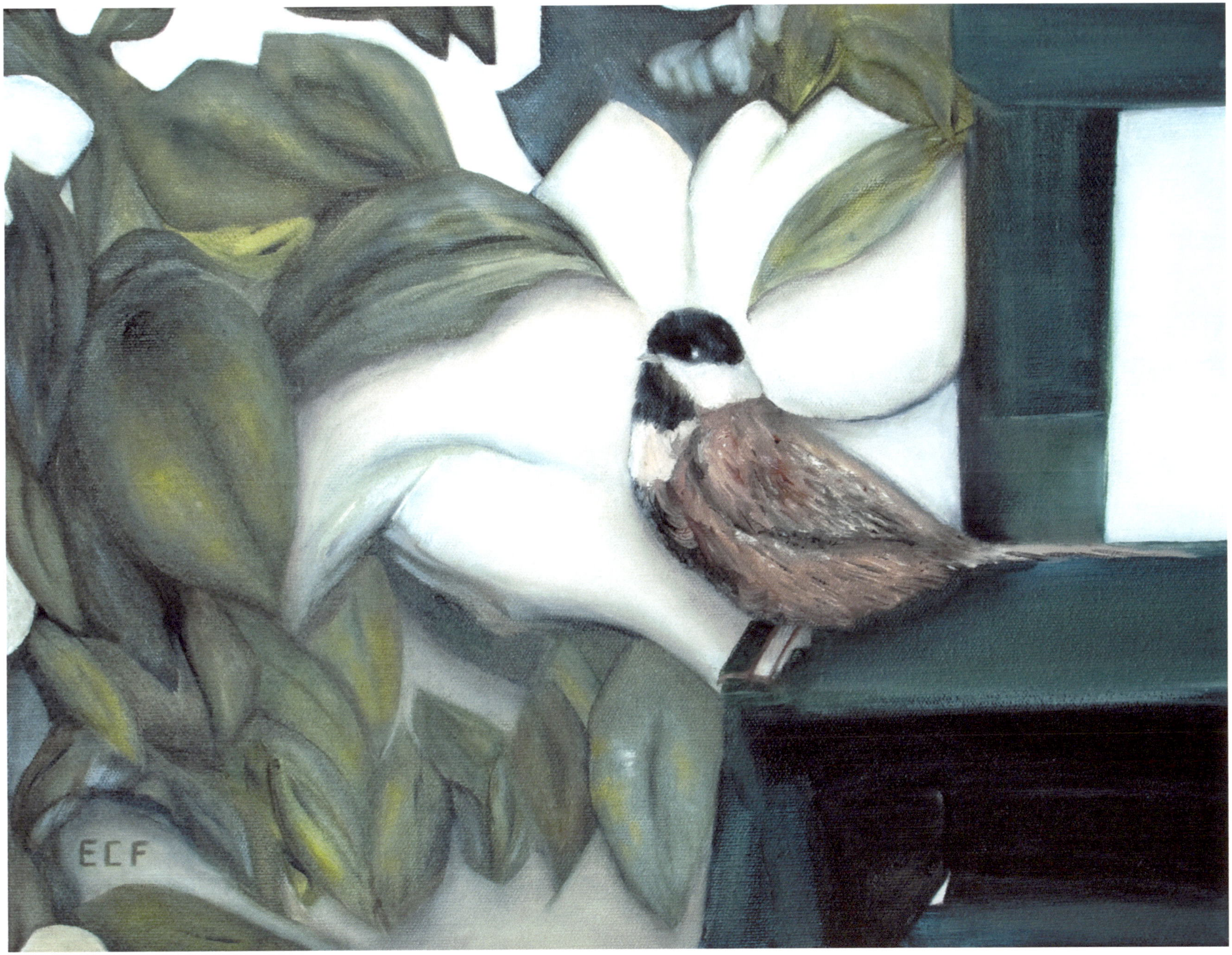

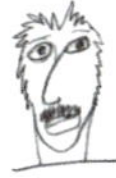

E. C. Flickinger, *The Bird*, 2011
Oil on canvas, 16 x 12 inches

Wondrous Sky

Wondrous Sky inspired the cover of *Adam's Journal: A Novel* by E. C. Flickinger.

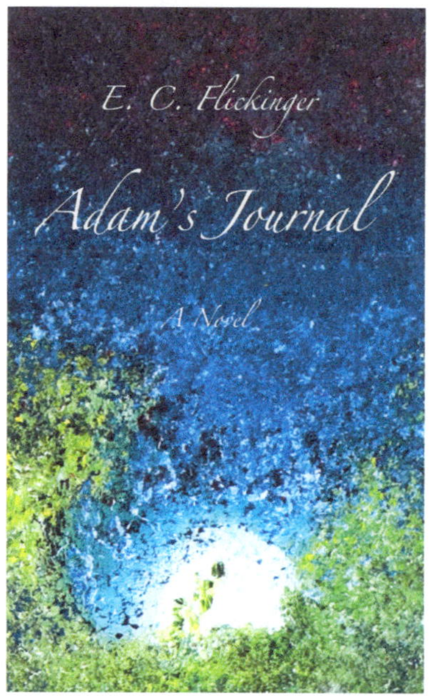

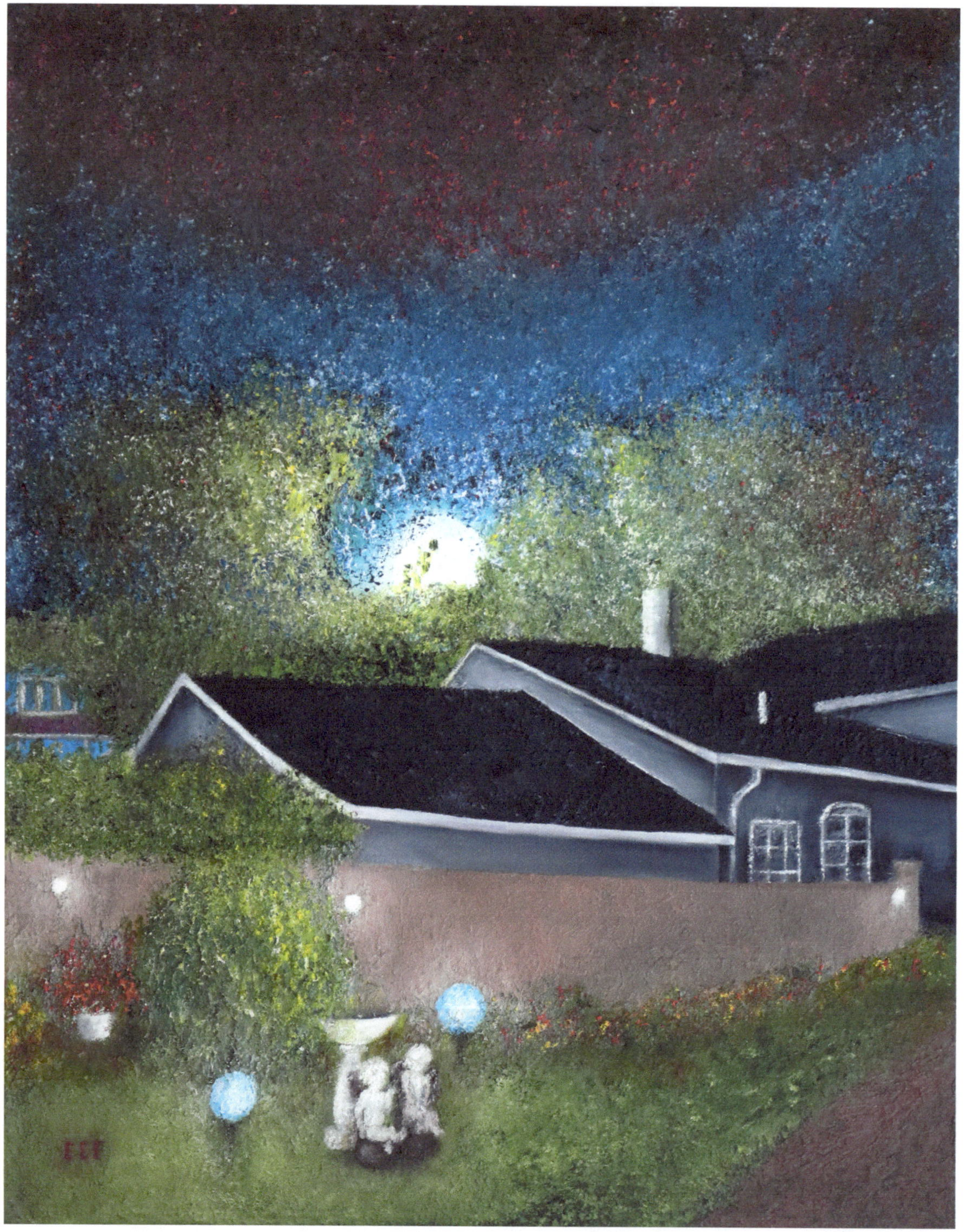

E. C. Flickinger
Wondrous Sky, 2016
Oil on canvas
16 x 20 inches

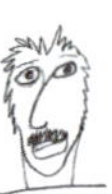

Sarah

Sarah was born in October of 1984 in Kingston, New York. As a child, she developed a keen appreciation of art while visiting her grandfather's studio, located in a suburb of Pittsburgh, Pennsylvania.

After expanding her skills under the direction of Saugerties, New York artist and instructor, Kristy Bishop, Sarah chose to attend The University of North Carolina in Greensboro. She earned a Bachelor of Fine Arts degree in Design in 2005.

In 2009, while working as a photographer and graphic designer, Sarah completed her Master of Fine Arts program in Documentary Photography from The Academy of Art University in San Francisco. Her thesis, "An Appreciation: North Carolina Century Farms," afforded visits throughout the state's one hundred counties to preserve those families' rich histories.

Sarah enjoys volunteering for organizations that support diversity, inclusion, and arts education. She served on the board of directors for Philadelphia's Allens Lane Art Center from 2017-2019.

Sarah recently contributed as a graphic designer and editor on Dr. Rob Brosh's "Rock History: A Musician's Perspective" (DDG Publishing).

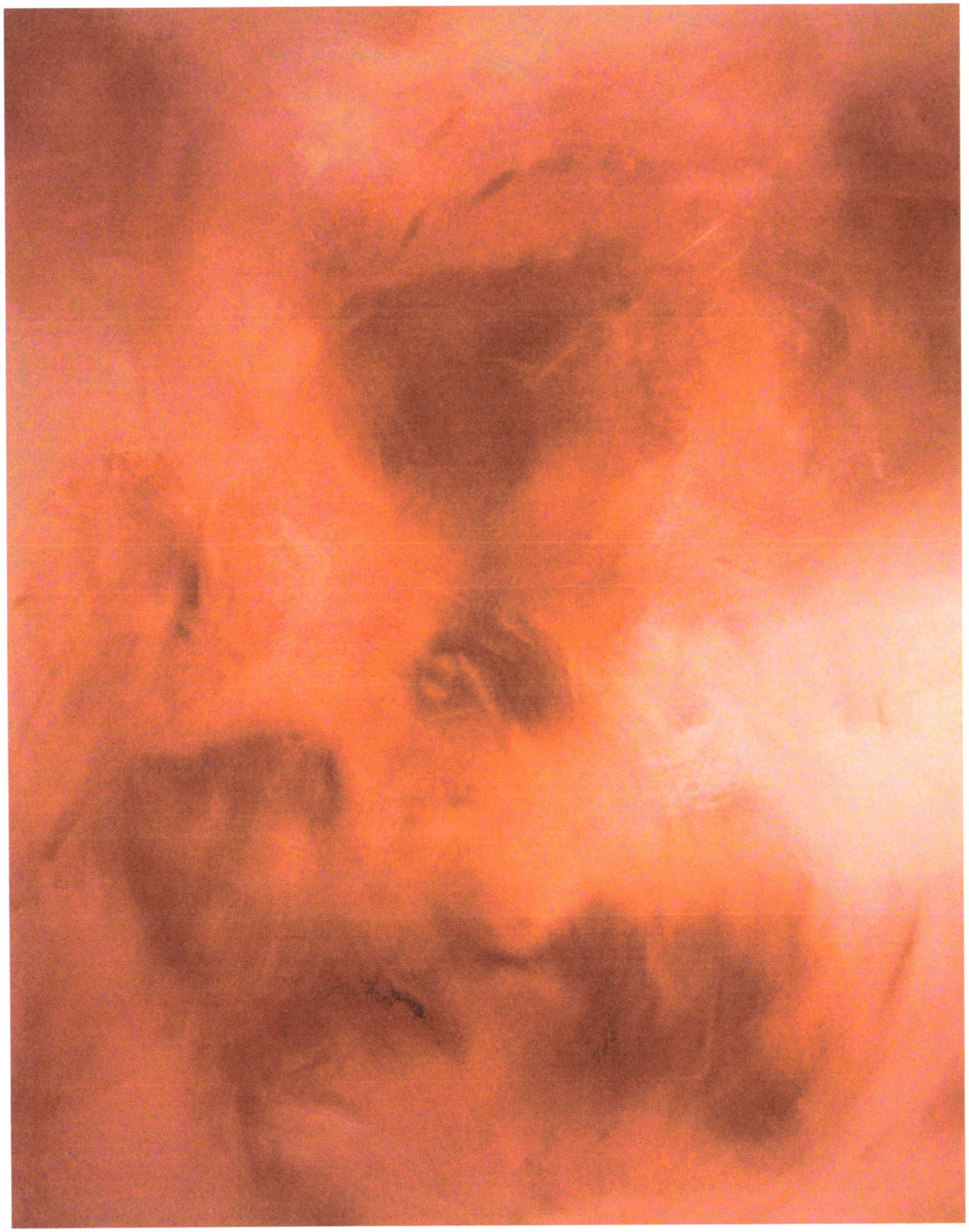

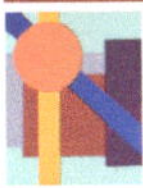

Sarah F. Wimberley, *Faces*, 2005, Mural

43

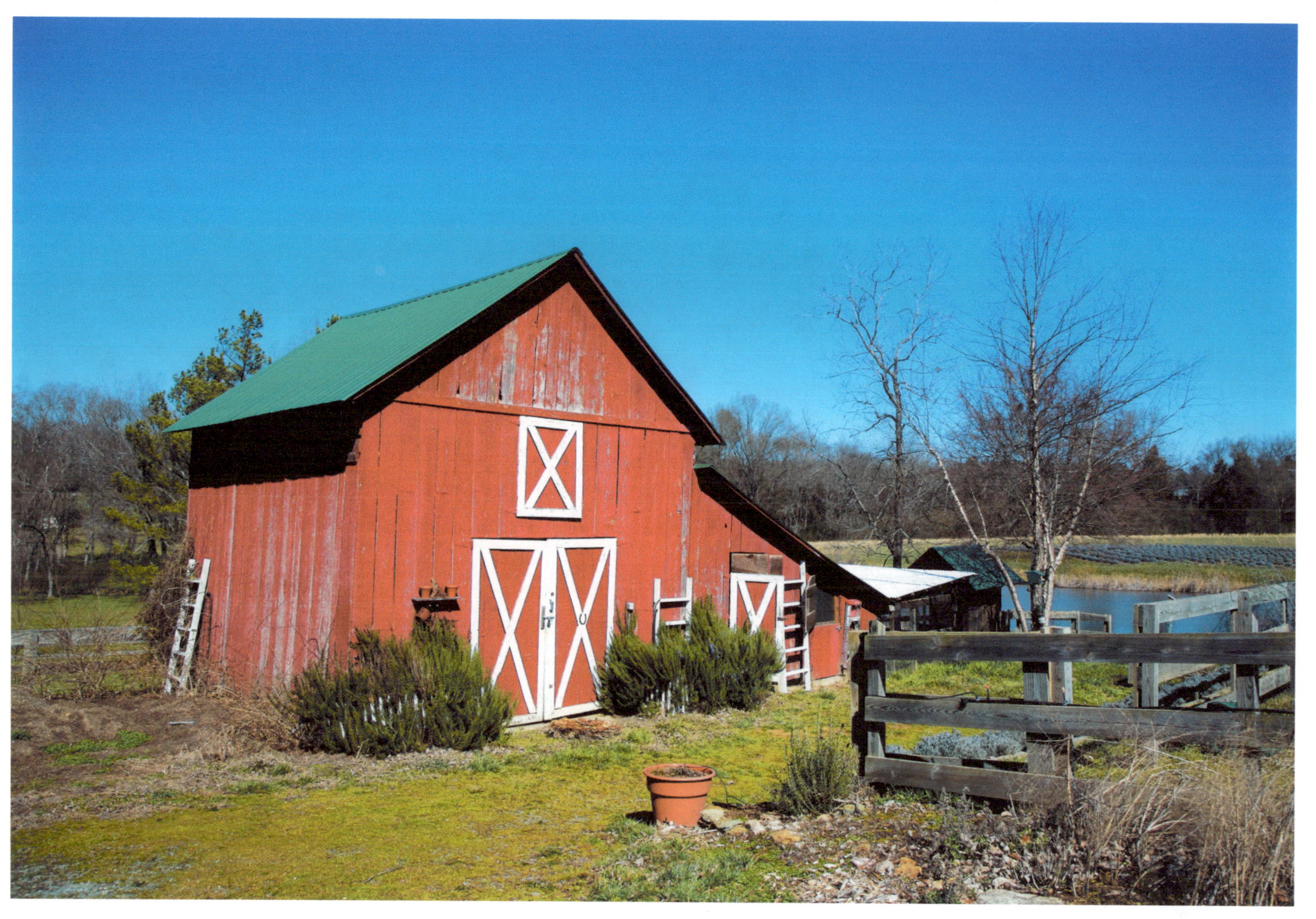

Sarah F. Wimberley
Unnamed Lavender Farm, c. 2007
Digital photography
Piedmont Region, NC

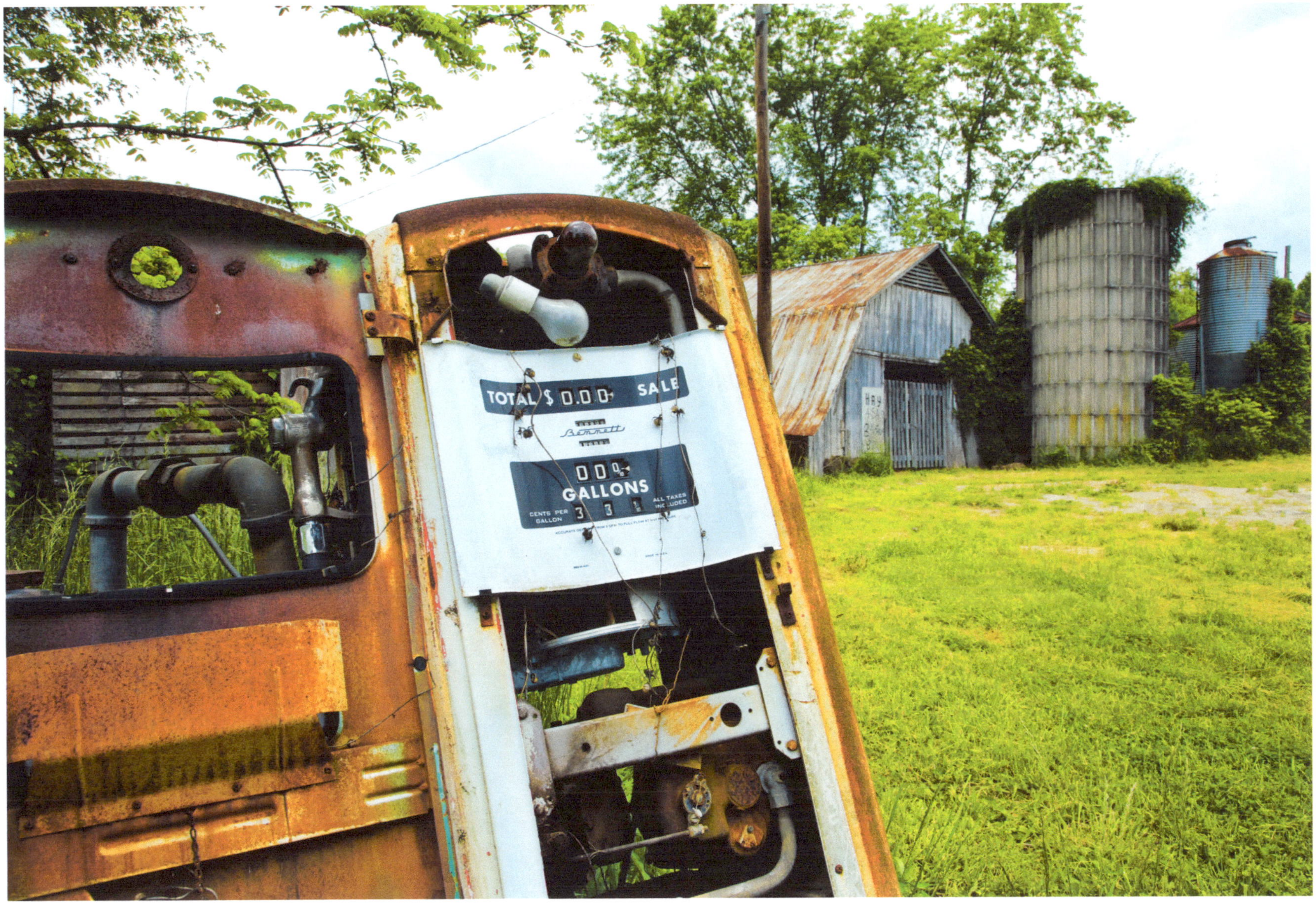

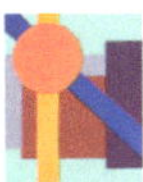

Sarah F. Wimberley
33 Cents a Gallon, c. 2007
Digital photography
Horse Shoe, Henderson County, NC

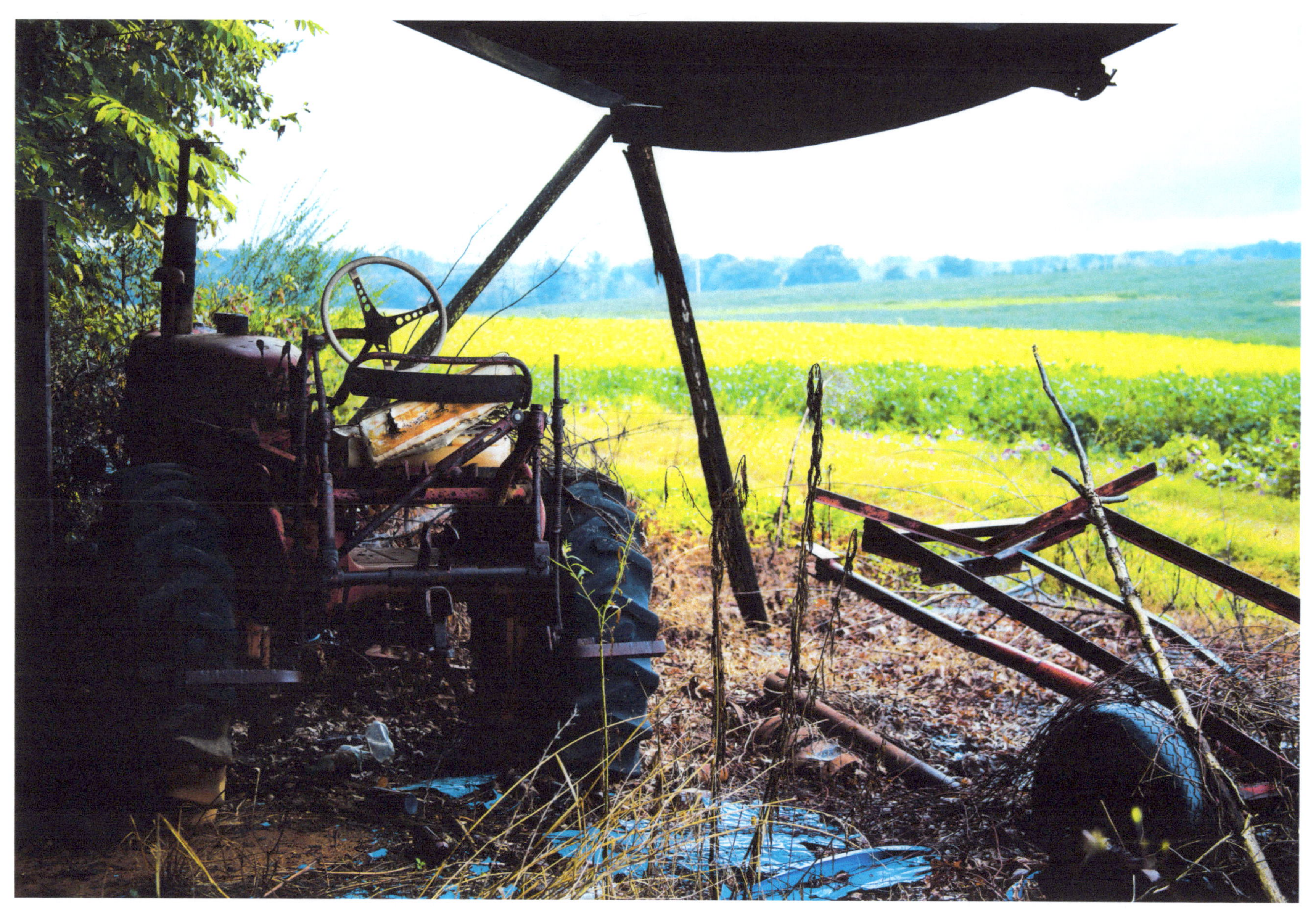

Sarah F. Wimberley
Gone But Not Forgotten, c. 2007
Digital photography
Ararat, Surry County, NC

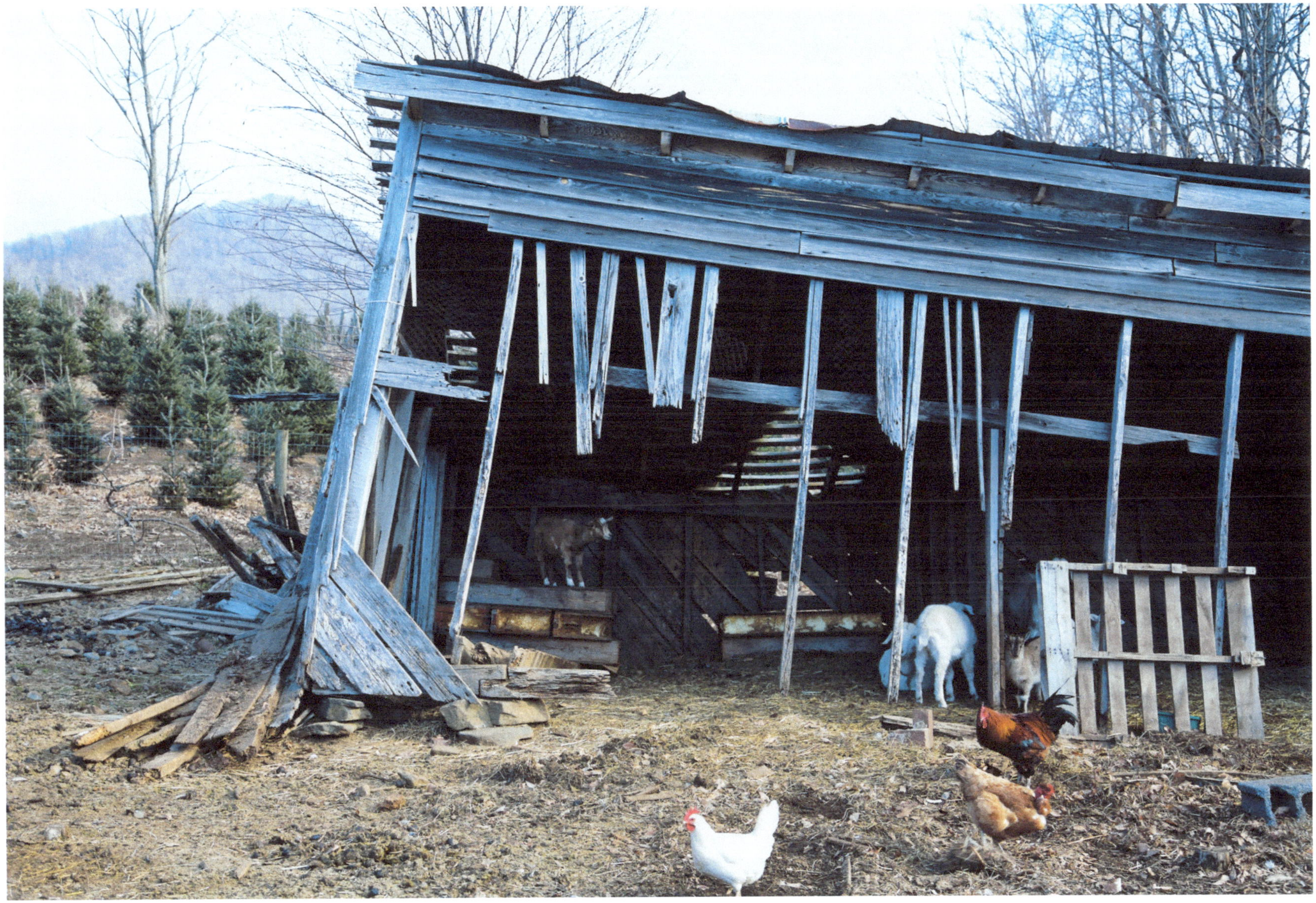

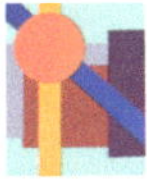

Sarah F. Wimberley
It Was Worth The Drive, c. 2007
Digital photography
Western Region, NC

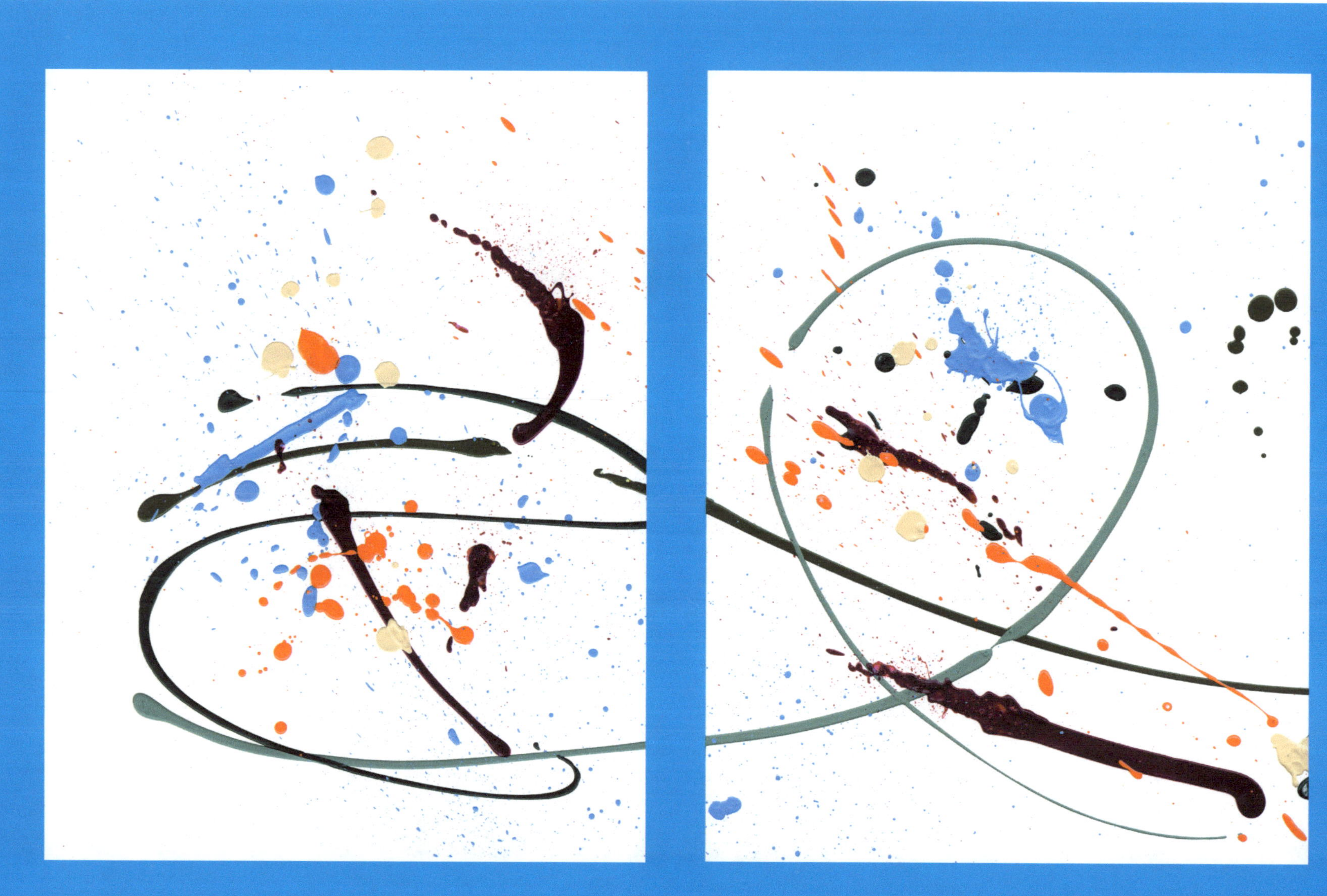

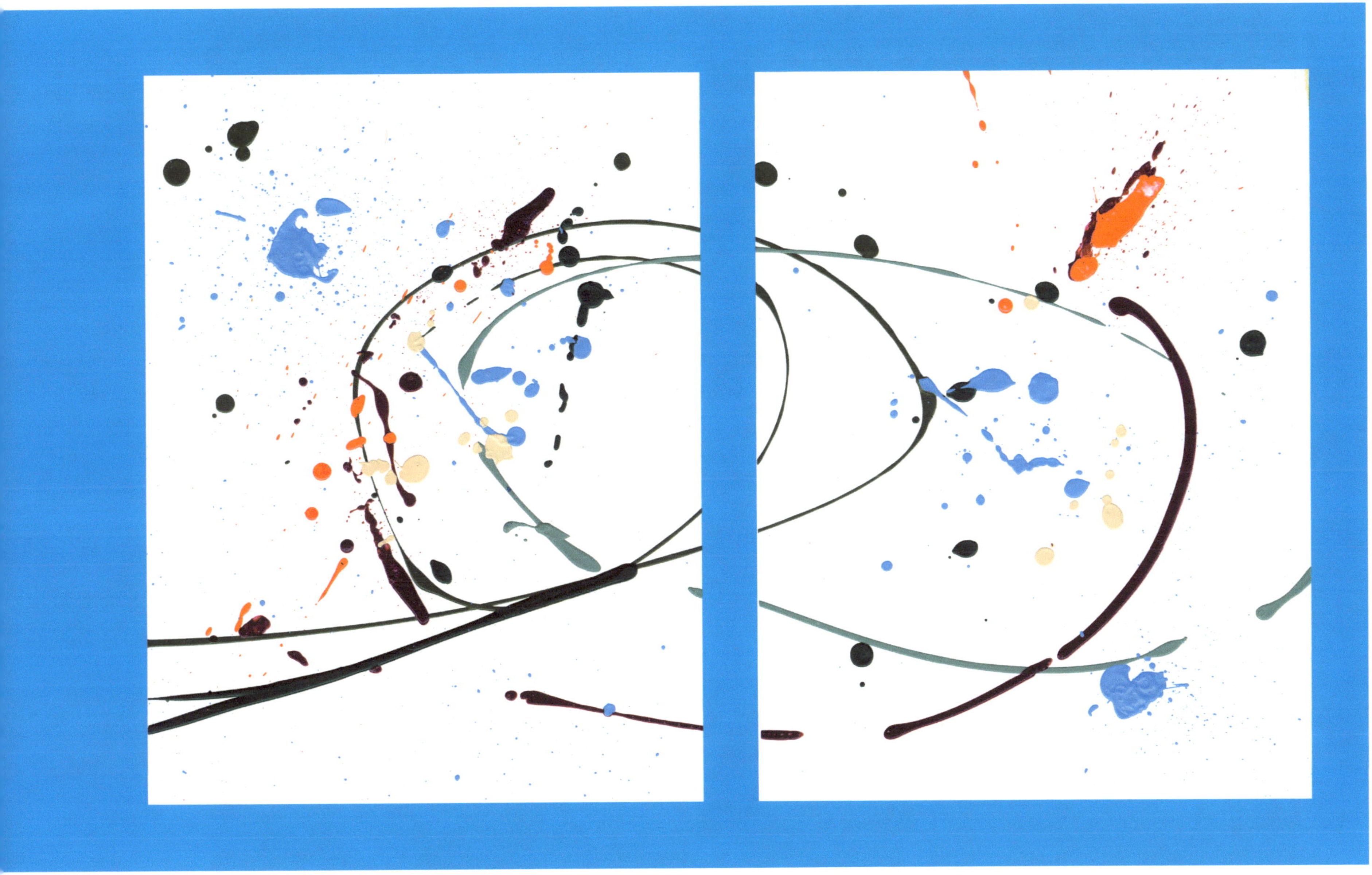

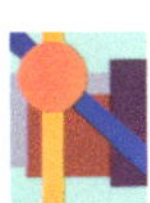

Sarah F. Wimberley
Here We Go, 2005
Acrylic on paper
Four 11 x 14-inch panels

49

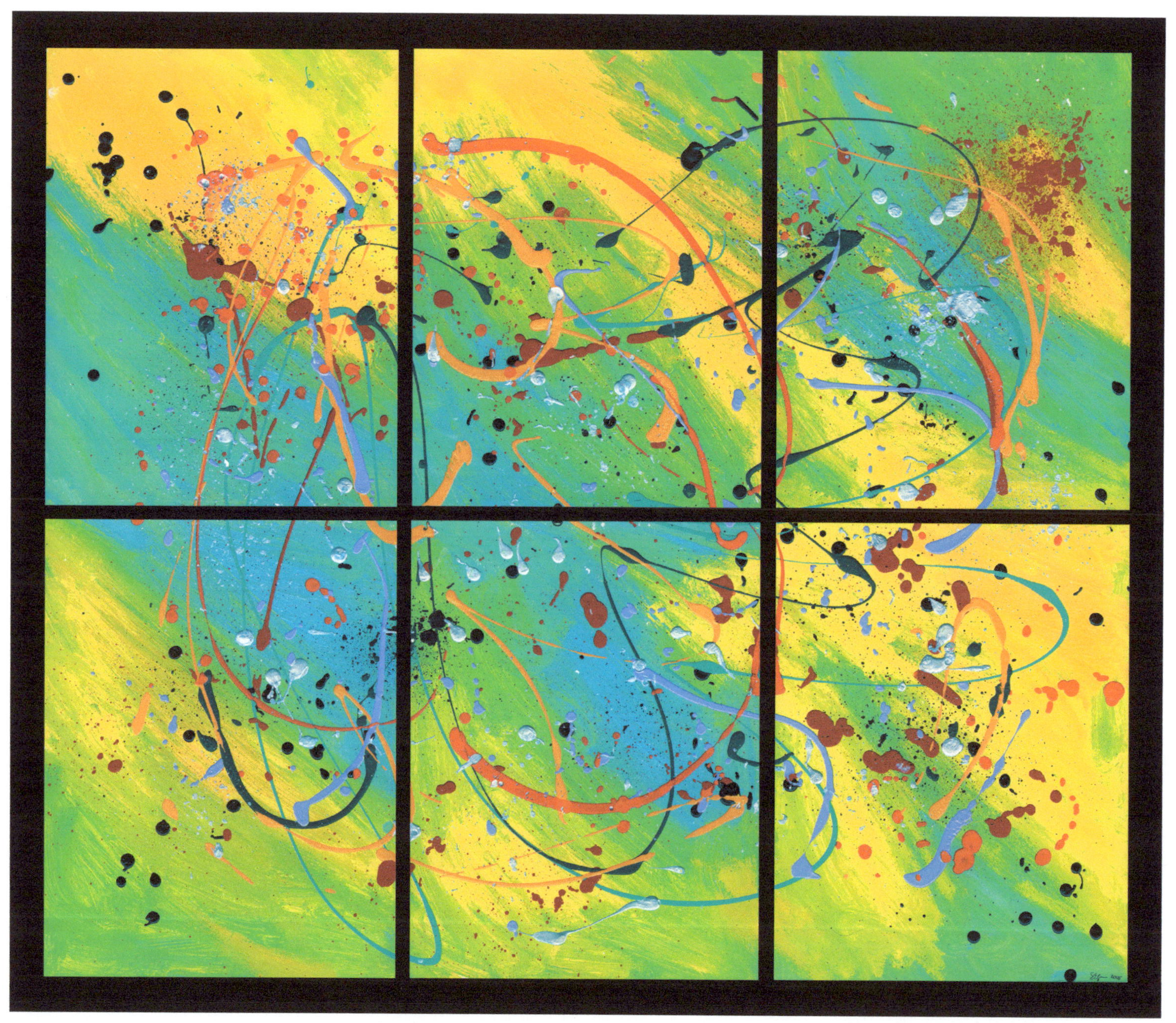

Sarah F. Wimberley, *Chaos*, 2005
Acrylic on paper, six 11 x 14-inch panels

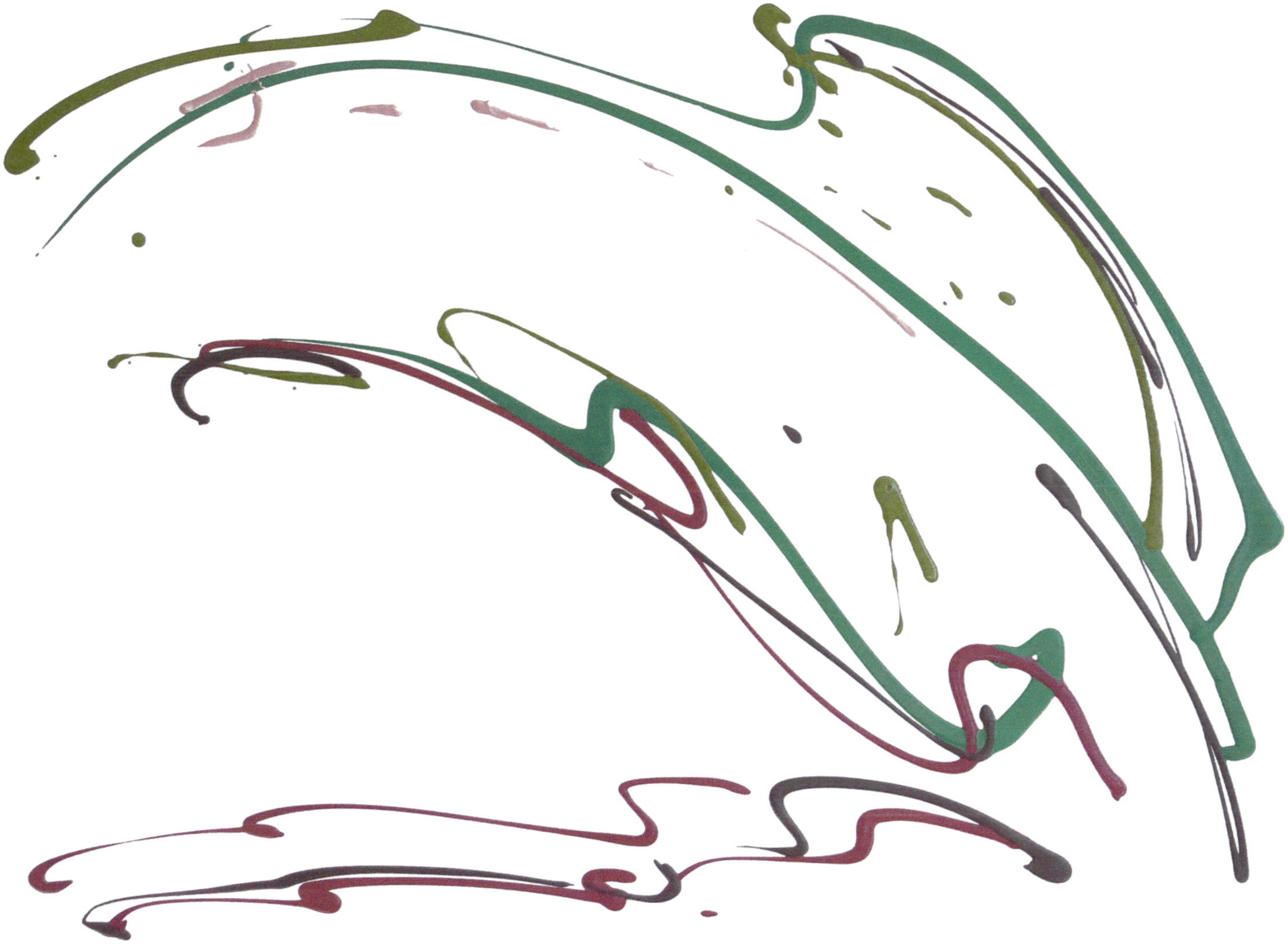

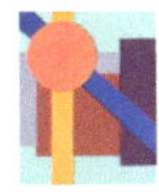

Sarah F. Wimberley, *Leaf*, 2005
Acrylic on canvas, 30 x 22 inches

Olivia

Olivia Marguerite Wimberley was born in Philadelphia in April of 2014. She enjoys painting, drawing, and playing outside. Earlier today, she searched for worms with her younger brother, Jack.

Olivia is learning to read. She will proudly tell you that both her name and Oma's name start with the same letter: *O*.

"Oma is my grandmother. Bub is my grandfather. Bub starts with *B*."

Olivia has bold fashion sense; her favorite colors are pink and green.

Olivia loves to travel on family vacations and can't wait for the next sleepover at her grandparent's house.

Olivia attends Green Lane Preschool and is looking forward to kindergarten next year.

Olivia currently lives in Philadelphia with her parents, Sarah and Sean, and her brother, Jackson.

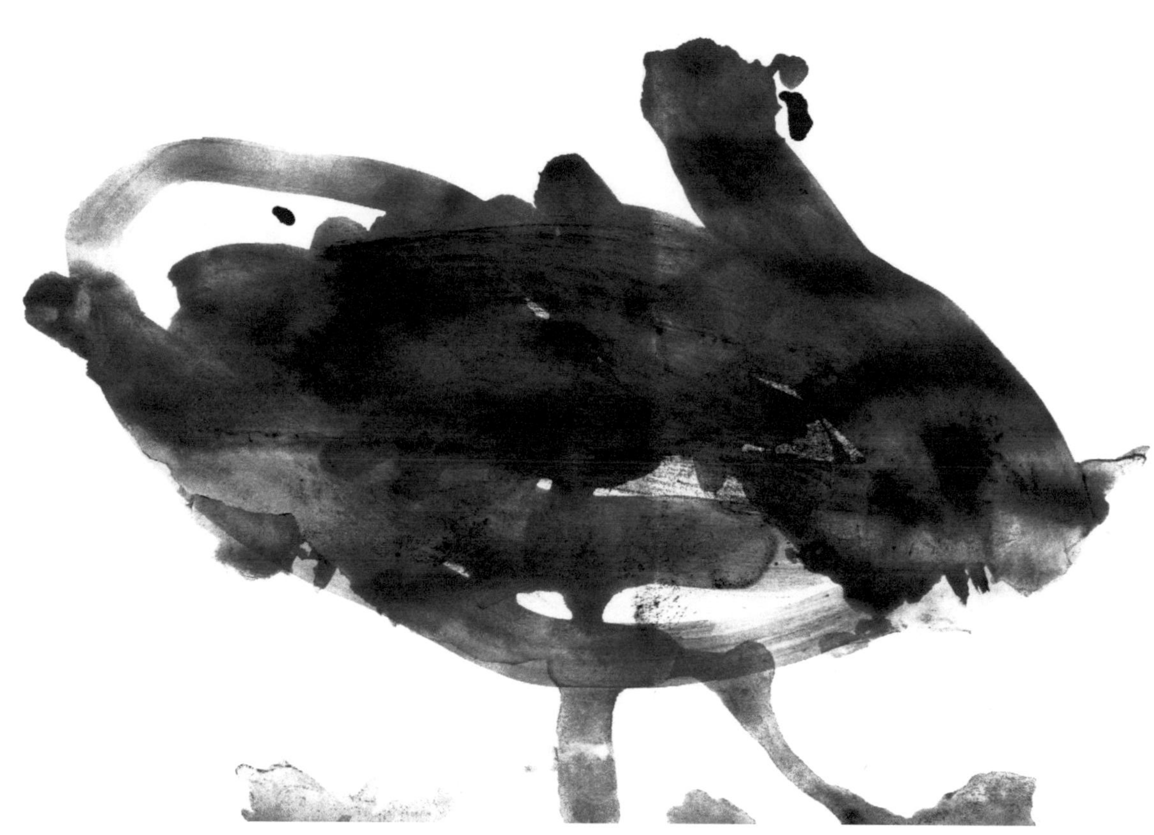

Olivia M. Wimberley
Pigeon, 2018
Watercolor on paper, 14 x 8.5 inches
Age 4

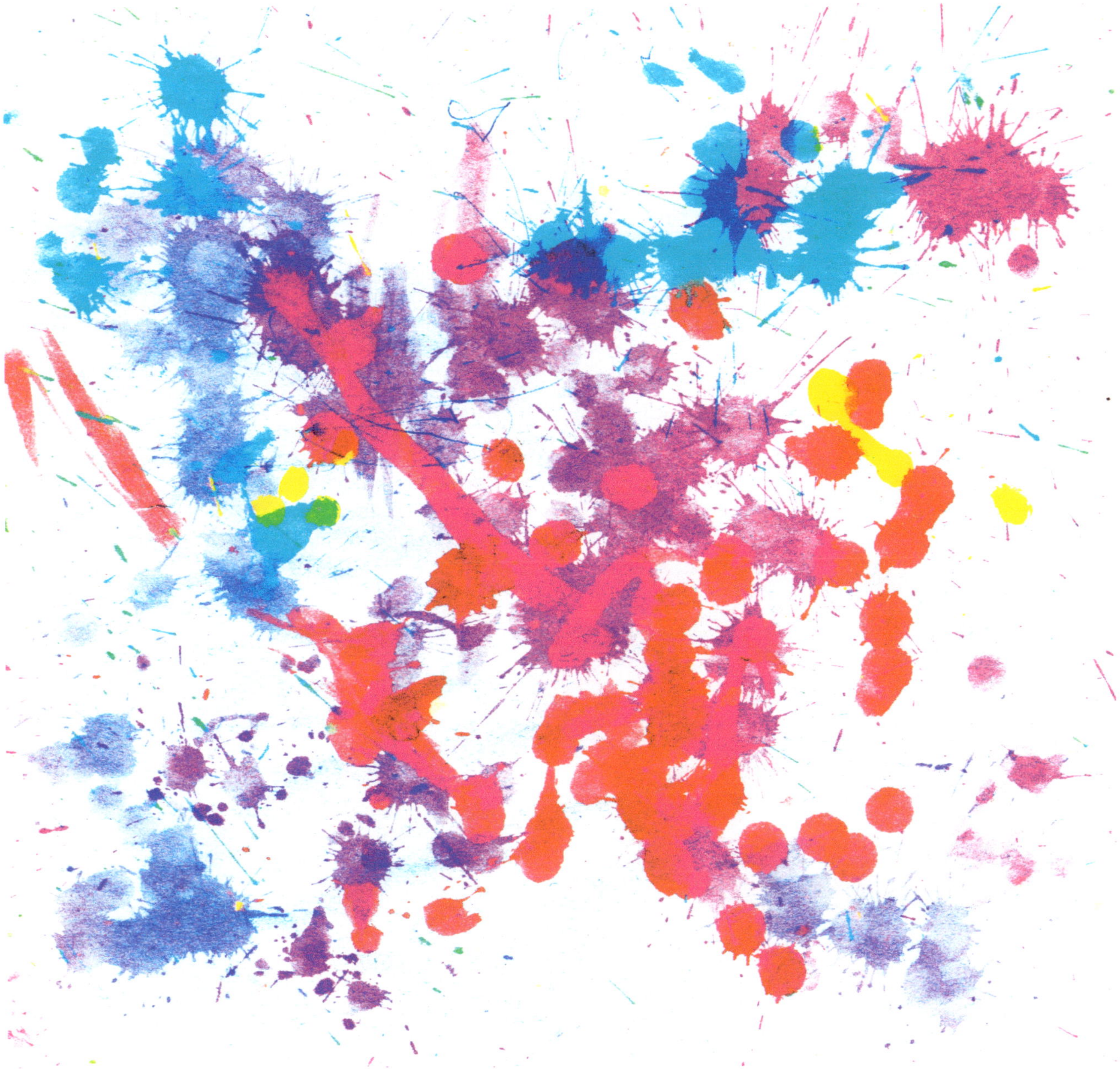

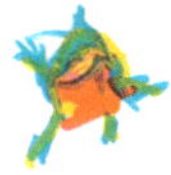

Olivia M. Wimberley
At Age Two, 2016
Watercolor on paper, 12 x 11 inches
Age 2

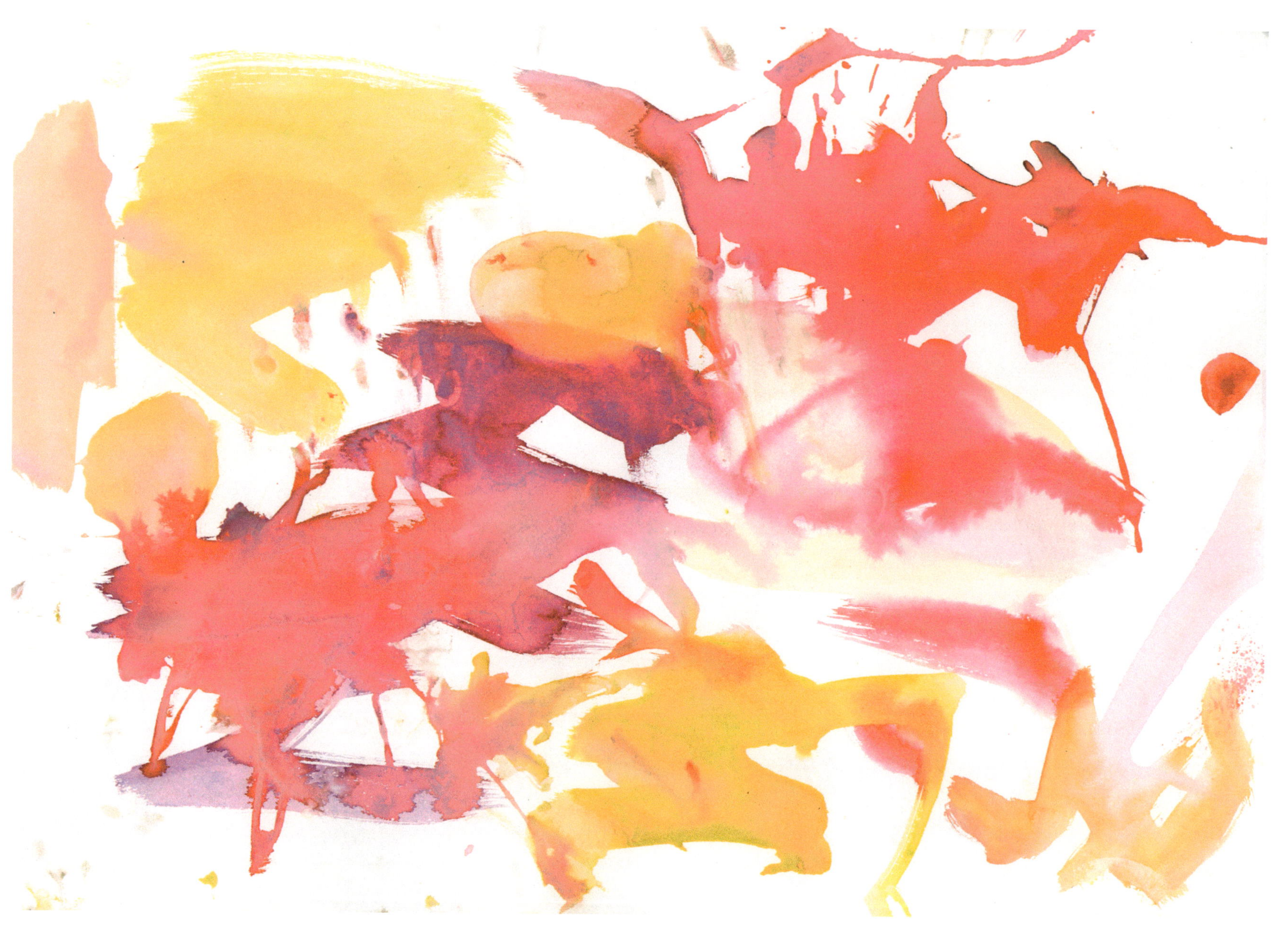

Olivia M. Wimberley
Playground, 2016
Watercolor on paper, 17 x 12 inches
Age 2

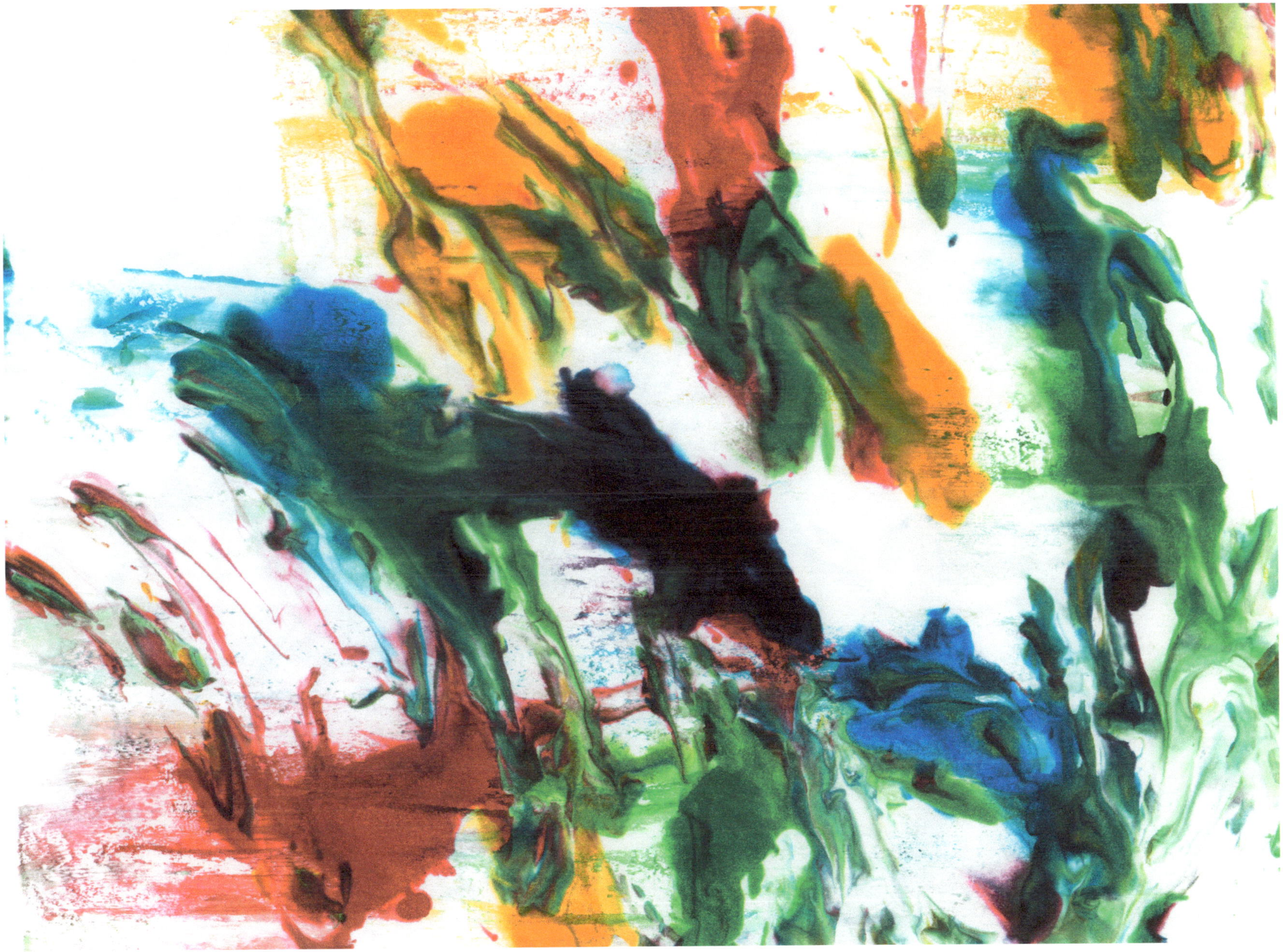

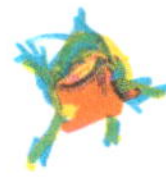

Olivia M. Wimberley
Park, 2017
Watercolor on paper, 11 x 8.5 inches
Age 3

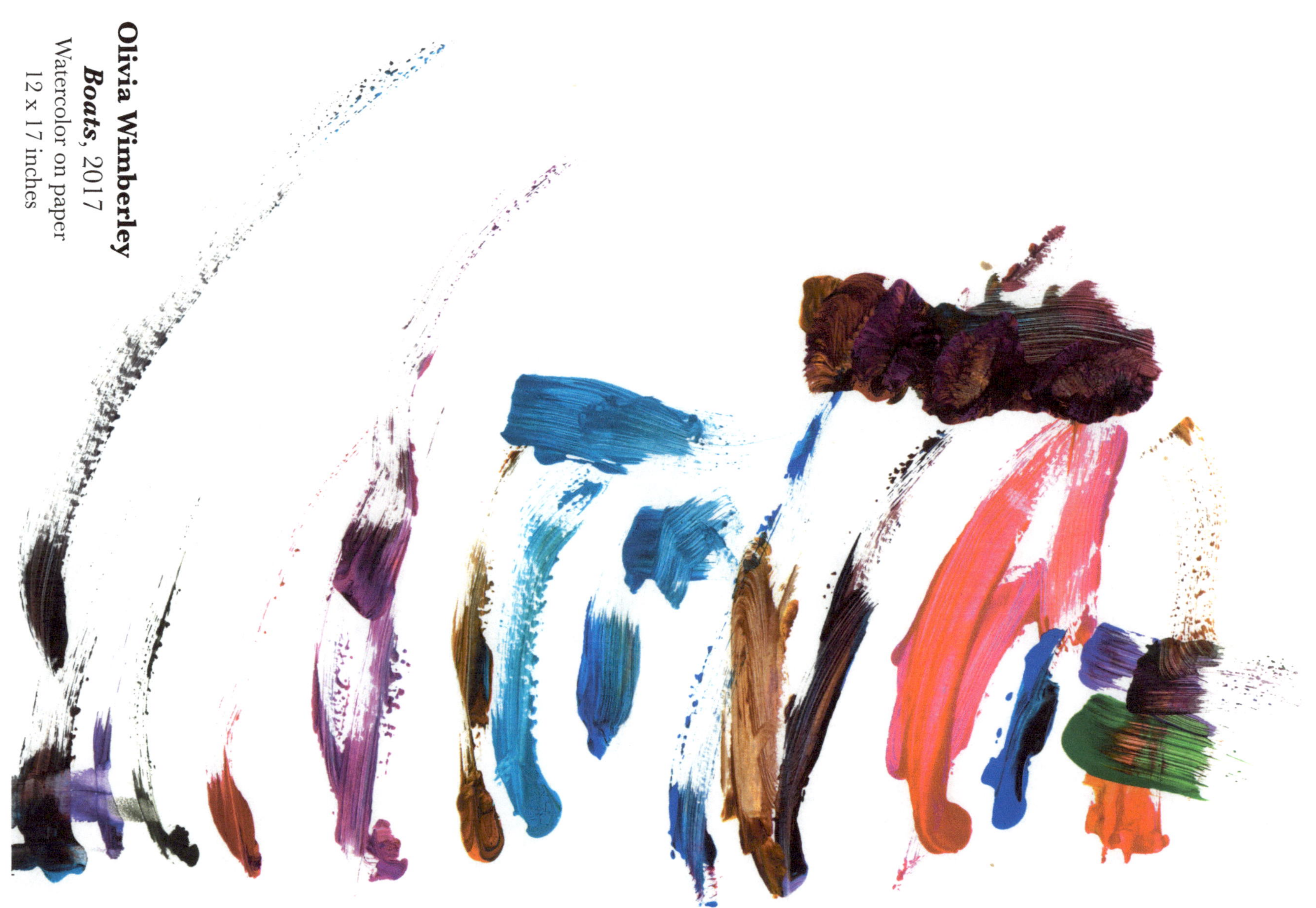

Olivia M. Wimberley
Waiting, 2017
Watercolor on paper, 17 x 12 inches
Age 3

56

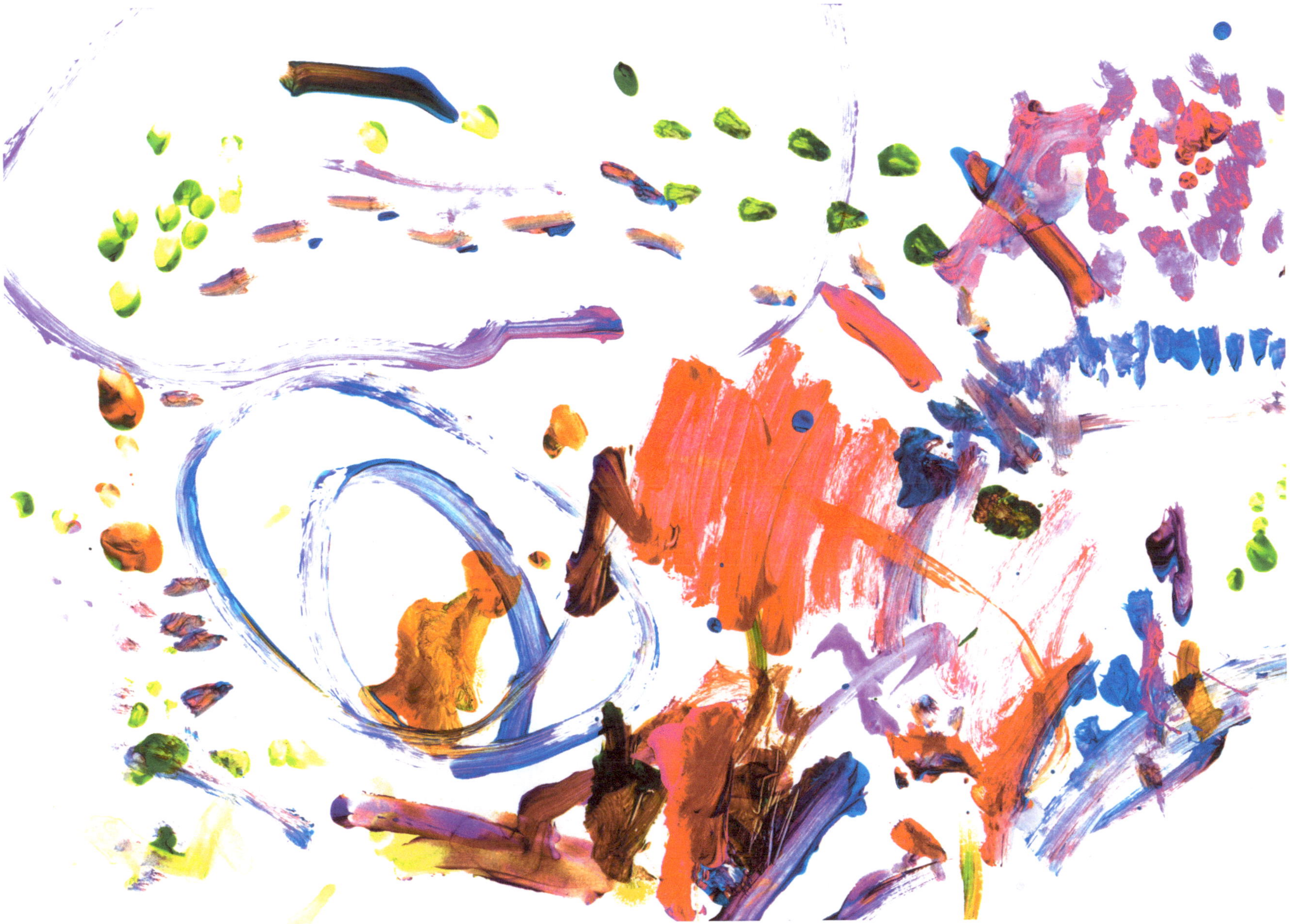

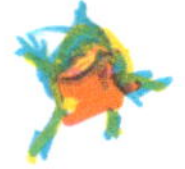

Olivia M. Wimberley
Go Climb The Mountain, 2017
Watercolor on paper, 17 x 12 inches
Age 3

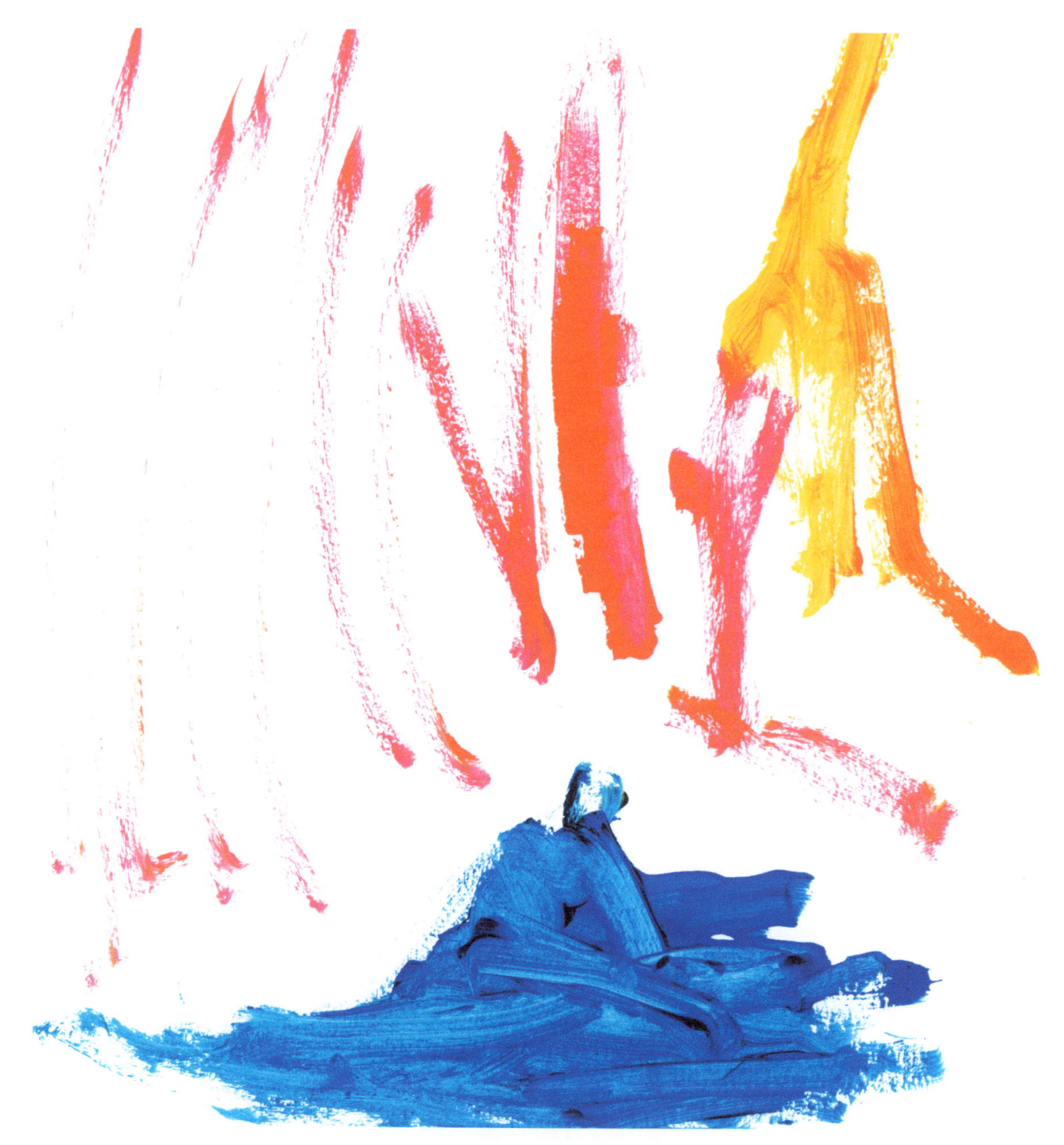

Olivia M. Wimberley
Boat, 2018
Watercolor on paper, 12 x 14 inches
Age 4

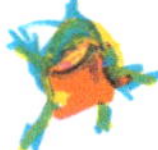

Olivia M. Wimberley
Fly, 2018
Watercolor on paper, 17 x 12 inches
Age 4

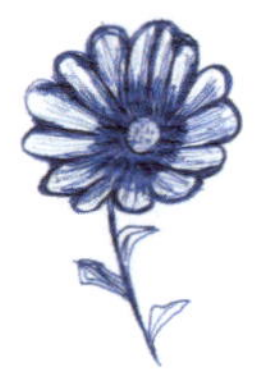

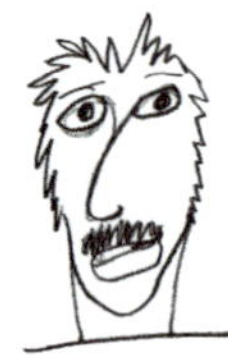

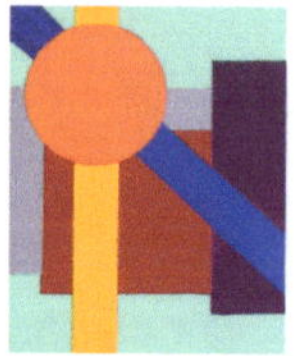

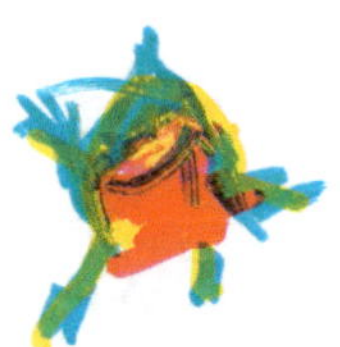

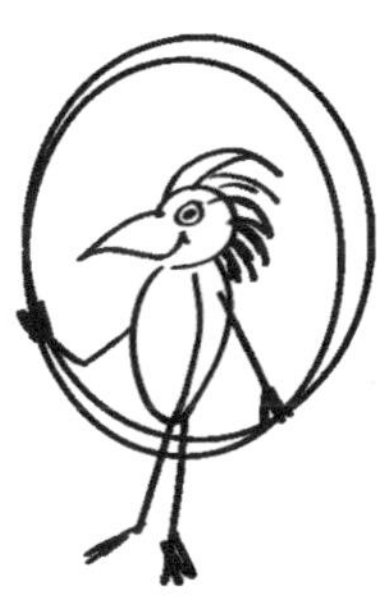

A Grackle Book